SEL

GAME

Published in 2005 by:
The Gallery Publications
P.O. Box 3181, Zanzibar, Tanzania
e-mail: gallery@swahilicoast.com

Designed by Terence Fernandes
Proof editing by Vanessa Beddoe

ISBN: 9987 667 46 5

The text reflects the private views of the authors only and not necessarily those of organizations they work for. Profits accruing to the authors from this publication are used for community programmes around the Reserve. The authors thank Deutsche Gesellschaft für Technische Zusammenarbeit (GTZ) for enabling them to accumulate the information contained in this travel guide during their work for that organisation in Tanzania. We also thank Benson Kibonde, Barbara Baldus, Celia and Rob Mills and Fiona Reed for assistance.

SELOUS
GAME RESERVE

Rolf D. Baldus • Ludwig Siege • Javed Jafferji

Published by
Gallery Publications

CONTENTS

Left: Cutting through the jungle with a golden track. The Rufiji at sunset

Next pages:

Arial view overlooking the stunning Rufiji Delta

Elephants crossing the river at sunset

Safari in style - champagne breakfast on a sandbank

Wild dogs

Securing the lion population in the Selous

FOREWORD

This is the fourth Selous Travel Guide written by the authors. Compared to the previous guides it has been extended, updated and illustrated with new photos by Javed Jafferji. The first guide appeared in the early nineties, as at that time there was no guidebook for the visitor to the Selous. 14,000 copies, one non-approved reprint and texts pirated for other publications have proved that the previous travel guides were recognized as the only reliable source of information for visitors to the northern sector of the largely unknown Selous Game Reserve. Unfortunately, many general travel guide books covering Tanzania or East Africa as a whole have been found to be unreliable as far as the Selous is concerned.

The authors have worked in or with the Selous for a total of over 20 years. They are proud to have been - together with their Tanzanian colleagues and friends - part of the rehabilitation and recovery of this great protected area. Tanzania deserves praise for setting aside such a large area of land for wildlife and nature to flourish in.

Left: Giraffes checking out the photographer

Germany and other countries have all played their part in the past to contribute to the survival of this World Heritage Site, which is Africa's largest and oldest protected area. The management and protection of the Selous is nowadays mainly financed from the Reserve's own income. All fees paid by visitors flow directly back into the Selous.

In the past a number of ill-conceived projects which would have endangered these wildlands have been avoided, but there are currently new dangers on the horizon. Prospecting for gem stones has been permitted and, if this plan were to go ahead; the visitor might soon find artisanal Tanzanite diggers and excavating machinery tearing the hills apart at Beho Beho. There is international agreement that mining must not be allowed in World Heritage Sites like the Selous. On another front, some think that an easy way to solve the notorious water supply problems of the capital Dar es Salaam is by building a dam across the Ruvu at Kidunda, thereby destroying the great wetland between the northern boundary and the villages south of the Ulugurus. This stretch of land is not only a Wildlife Management Area where those villages protect and utilize the game on their land,

but at the same time an indispensable dry season refuge for elephants, buffaloes, wildebeest, zebras and impalas from the Selous. If this dam were built across the Ruvu River and the "Gonabis wetland" flooded, many thousand animals which normally roam the Northern Selous would lose part of their habitat and be gone forever. We trust and are optimistic that the conservation minded Government of Tanzania will not allow these projects to proceed.

The authors want every visitor to spend fabulous days in the wildlands stretching between the Rufiji and the Mgeta Rivers, along the Lakes, the Western hills and Stiegler's Gorge. Wonderful tented camps and lodges, all with their own particular safari style, await the traveller when returning from a long and dusty day in the bush. Enjoy the Selous! It is one of Tanzania's great wild places. It is less disturbed and has more game than it had one hundred years ago. Let us keep it like that – and Safari Njema!

Left: A typical vista at Selous
Top: Yellow-billed Stork
Next page: The best way to see Stiegler's Gorge - by boat

THE HISTORY OF THE RESERVE

The Time of the Explorers

Stone implements used by an unknown, early people have been found in the Reserve. More recently, the Reserve was on the route of caravans bringing slaves and ivory from the interior to the coast. In the middle of the nineteenth century the village of Kisaki, which is now on the Northern border of the Reserve, was a junction between two major trade routes, and large caravans of some thousand people regularly passed through during the dry season. Explorers like Burton and Speke (1859-60) or von Decken (1860) crossed the region. The Scot Johnston died at Beho Beho in 1879 while trying to reach Lake Tanganyika. We have tried to find his grave on several expeditions, but the wilderness has reclaimed it. These brave adventurers found only few people living in isolated villages and separated from each other by vast stretches of bush. A general scarcity of game is also reported in contemporary accounts. Johnston's companion Thomson, who managed to

Left: Young lioness resting in the heat of the day

reach the great lakes in the interior and returned home via Masailand had to go to the zoo in Edinburgh in order to see his first elephant.

On July 7th, 1905 Wilhelm Kuhnert (1868 - 1926), who was one of the first European artists to observe and paint African animals in the wild, crossed the Mgeta River into what is now the Selous. In his unpublished diary he describes the area around Beho Beho as the most beautiful steppe imaginable and Lake Tagalala as an outstanding, scenic place. Three years later the German naturalist Hans Schomburgk hunted in the Northern Selous, and his books contain photos of the wildlife along the Rufiji River.

Maji-Maji and World War I

In 1905 the Maji-Maji insurrection against the German colonial government swept through the Southern part of the country. "Maji" is the Kiswahili word for water and it was 'magic' water which gave that early anti-colonial struggle its name. Its source was

Left: Caravans brought ivory and slaves fom the interior
Top: Scenes from the Rufiji River by Wilhelm Kuhnert

reputed to be close to the Rufiji River and it was believed to make the warriors invulnerable.

Fighting returned to the Reserve in the First World War. The light German cruiser "Königsberg" found shelter in the Rufiji delta about 100km east of Mtemere. After it was sunk by the British Royal Navy, the German forces removed the ten 4.1 inch guns, put them on wheels and hauled them through a good part of the East African campaign. In 1917 the German forces under General von Lettow-Vorbeck clashed with the British near Beho Beho where the English explorer, Frederick Courteney Selous, met his death in action. His friend, J.G. Millais, provided in 1919 the following description of the event:

"Our force moved out from Kisaki early on the morning of January 4th 1917, with the object of attacking and surrounding a considerable number of German troops which was encamped along the low hills east of Beho-Beho (Sugar Mountain) N.E. of the road that led from Kisaki S.E. to the Rufiji River, distant some 13 miles from the enemy's position. The low hills occupied by the Germans were densely covered with thorn-bush and the visibility to the west was not good. Nevertheless, they soon realised the danger of their position when they detected a circling movement on the part of the 25th Royal Fusiliers, which had been detailed to stop them on the road leading S.E., the only road, in fact, by which they could retreat. They must have retired early, for their forces came to this point at the exact moment when the leading company of Fusiliers, under Captain Selous, reached the same point. Heavy firing on both sides then commenced, and Selous at once deployed his company, attacked the Germans which greatly outnumbered him, and drove them back into the bush. It was at this moment that Selous was struck dead from a shot to the head."

An eye-witness who stood on his left side when it happened later narrated that Ramathani, Selous' gunbearer for 28 years, jumped up with red bloodshot eyes, regardless of the bullets, and shot two snipers in the trees. *"He then lay down, stretched his arms over his master and cried like a baby."*

Frederick Courteney Selous (pronounce: seloo with final "s" silent) was born in 1851 as son of a chairman of the London Stock Exchange. His ambition was to follow his boyhood hero David Livingstone to Africa, which he finally achieved in 1871. He hunted and explored Matabeleland and served as a guide for Cecil Rhodes in opening up what is now Zimbabwe for European settlers. A keen naturalist, hunter and early conservationist, he wrote many books about his adventures and

Left: Frederick Courteney Selous

natural history, some of which became bestsellers in Victorian England. When this veteran of the Matabele wars took up arms again in the First World War at the age of 64, he was already a living legend and one of the greatest outdoorsman of his time - a sort of British "Buffalo Bill".

He joined the 25th Battalion, The Royal Fusiliers, in Nairobi and helped to chase the greatly outnumbered German Schutztruppe under von Lettow-Vorbeck slowly down towards Southern Tanzania. It was said that Selous never rode a yard of the way but marched with his men who suffered greatly from disease and the hostile climate. When finally, in late 1916, they drove the Germans out of the fortified village at Kisaki, only 60 men of the original 1166 strong force were fit for duty. In the evening, when his men collapsed into their wet tents and trenches, Captain Selous took out his butterfly net and collected specimens. He also continued hunting during the campaign as a kudu trophy which is still in the family shows.

1896 - The Kaiser Creates Africa's First Protected Area

The indigenous population of East Africa had certain "sacred forests" and similar areas where hunting was not allowed. The first modern National Park was Yellowstone in the USA which was established in 1872. The first formal reservation of wild lands for recre-

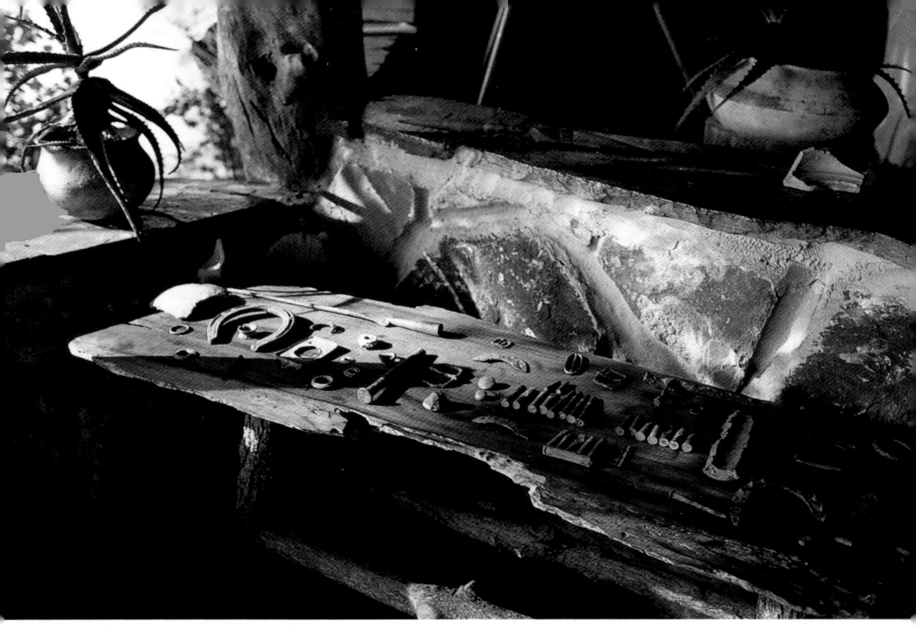

ational purposes, protection and research in Africa was the Selous. In 1896 the German Governor von Wissmann on behalf of his Majesty, Kaiser Wilhelm II, banned hunting in the area between the Mgeta and Rufiji and declared it a reserve. What is now the main tourist circuit in the northern sector of the Selous and the focus of this travel guide became thus the first protected area in Africa, two years earlier than the Krueger National Park of South Africa. Later the stretch between the Ruaha, Kilombero and Ulanga Rivers in the west and two other areas in the east near Liwale were also declared game reserves. A wildlife conservation law was enacted and enforced. According to recently discovered manuscripts, the German wildlife photographer and author Carl Georg Schillings (1865 – 1921) drafted a wildlife policy combining protection with sustainable use of game, which is amazingly modern in content.

To this day the Selous is called "shamba la bibi" by the local people living around the Reserve. This means "the field of the lady" and it is said that the name stems from the German Kaiser Wilhelm, who presented the game reserves as a birthday gift to his wife. However, we have not been able to find any written evidence for this and believe it is just a charming folk tale.

Left: Dead trees in Lake Tagalala
Top: Cartridges and other remains of World War I battlefields at Beho Beho

After the war German East Africa became the British Protectorate of Tanganyika, and the existing four protected areas were expanded. The conglomerate was named "Selous" in 1922 in memory of the great explorer who fell there in 1917.

During the 1930's and 1940's the administration of the Tanganyika Protectorate, in its fight against endemic sleeping sickness, moved the population away from tsetse-fly infected areas. The easiest way to prevent them from moving back was to add these wilderness areas to the already existing game reserve. Outside the protected area, up to three thousand elephants were shot every year because of their habit of destroying crops. The policy at that time was to protect the wildlife within the Reserve but to shoot problem animals outside.

Constantine Ionides, an eccentric Englishman and outstanding hunter based in Liwale, along with a handful of scouts, was responsible for elephant control and pro-

tection of wildlife for thousands of square kilometres, including the greater part of the Selous. He could not have been successful without the assistance of outstanding Tanzanian Game Officers like Mzee Madogo, who was re-employed by us in his late sixties to train the scouts and who died in 1996 in his beloved "shamba la bibi". Brian Nicholson, the last European Chief Warden also did a commendable job turning the Selous into a first-class game reserve. Brian, now retired to Australia, introduced safari hunting into the hitherto unused Reserve, as he needed substantial funds to finance the necessary infrastructure and antipoaching controls in the vast tracts of wilderness.

The last addition to the Selous was the southern bank of the Rufiji River during the Ujamaa villagisation campaign in 1974. Until then a regular bus service operated up to the southern bank opposite Kibambawe. The inhabitants of these villages were resettled along the Mloka - Mkongo road. However, the people had been deprived of fertile shambas, bush meat and first class fishing waters and in this area poaching has posed a challenge to the Reserve's administration ever since.

The Poaching Crisis 1973 to 1990

When the Government introduced a hunting ban in 1973, the income from safari hunting fell to zero and the professional hunters moved out, leaving the Reserve open to the poachers. The decline began. It was enforced by the deep economic crisis which ensued as a consequence of President Julius Nyerere's African socialism. Some disastrous development projects did the rest. Efforts to build a dam and a hydroelectric scheme

Top: Hippos and crocodiles in Lake Zalakela

brought up to 2,000 workers to Stiegler's Gorge. The many rhinos in that area were consequently poached out. In the early eighties in prospecting for oil, thousands of kilometres of straight cutlines were bulldozed through the heart of the Selous. The lines opened up formerly impenetrable thickets and served as comfortable highways for poaching gangs consisting of up to sixty people.

When the Reserve was declared a "World Heritage Site" in 1982 the massive slaughter of elephants had already begun, reducing their number from approx. 110,000 in 1976 to well under 30,000 in 1989. About 20 elephants died every day by the Kalashnikov assault rifles and the heavy guns of the poachers.

From the middle of the eighties, however, determined young wardens were put in charge of the Reserve again. With the help of

conservation organisations like the Frankfurt Zoological Society, the Worldwide Fund for Nature and the African Wildlife Foundation as well as the German Development Cooperation, and also assisted by the constructive policies of the Tanzanian Government, the Wildlife Division managed to reverse the trend. Nowadays the Selous Game Reserve is internationally recognised as one of the best managed protected areas in Africa. Wildlife populations including elephants have risen, most of them to maximum carrying capacity, and poaching within the Reserve is under control. It is unrealistic to hope that poaching can ever be totally stopped.

Recovery Under the Selous Conservation Programme

Since 1987 the Selous has received major support under a number of projects, in particular through the Tanzanian-German Development Cooperation. The most important joint activity was the Selous Conservation Programme (SCP). Support from Germany came through the Deutsche Gesellschaft für Technische Zusammenarbeit (GTZ). SCP came to an end at the end of 2003, by which time the scout force has been equipped, infrastructure rehabilitated and a management plan developed, which is now guiding the operation of the Reserve.

The Programme introduced the so called retention scheme, under which the Selous is allowed to retain half of all income generated. The total annual income generated in the Reserve currently amounts to well over US$3 million.

Top: Poaching for ivory tusks in the Reserve is now under control

The second component of Tanzanian-German cooperation was the development of the community conservation scheme. Amongst other problems, wild animals cause loss of life and damage to crops. Despite legal restrictions on hunting, the demand for meat in the villages and the lucrative markets in villages and in Dar es Salaam have caused commercial poachers to hunt meat illegally and in an uncontrolled way. This all has led to conflicts with the Selous administration.

It will be impossible to maintain protected areas in the future without providing benefits to the population living around them. In order to be successful, conservation has to be practiced 'with' and 'through' the people and not 'against' them.

The first villages were enrolled in the scheme in 1989, and there are now 51 in the Community Wildlife Management Programme. Villages designate parts of their land as Wildlife Management Areas, where agriculture is excluded and wildlife is protected. In exchange they are allowed to hunt a controlled number of animals for their own consumption. They employ and pay village game scouts, who patrol the areas and prevent illegal use. Over 300 such scouts are presently working in the bufferzones. This approach has been incorporated into the new Wildlife Policy of Tanzania and is implemented countrywide. Currently the legal framework is being set up to enable the villages to receive cash income from photographic and hunting tourism on their land.

There is evidence that poaching in the buffer zones - some of them prime wildlife areas - has decreased significantly, and that wildlife is now returning to areas where it has been absent for many years. Satellite based elephant research carried out by Tanzanian and German scientists has shown that there is an important genetic corridor between the Southern Selous and the Niassa Game Reserve in Mozambique. This so-called Selous-Niassa corridor will be better protected in cooperation with the rural communities living there. A new programme has started to achieve this goal. It will be conducted in informal coordination with the Mozambiquan wildlife managers on the other side of the border. German development assistance continues to support the village wildlife schemes around the Selous in cooperation with the Tanzanian authorities.

Left: Giraffe under the shade of Terminalia trees

Next page: Rufiji River at sunset

THE LARGEST PROTECTED DRY FOREST ECOSYSTEM IN AFRICA

The greater part of the northern sector of the Selous is earmarked for photographic tourism, and this is one of the most beautiful and game-rich areas in the whole ecosystem. The outer limit of this sector to the north is marked by the Mgeta River, just north of the Tazara railway, to the east by the Reserve boundary, to the west by Stiegler's Gorge and the road to Matambwe and to the south by the Rufiji River. This is the part of the Selous which is described in this guidebook. The other parts of the Reserve, which lie south of the Ruaha and Rufiji Rivers, are not developed for photographic tourism. As tourism is on the increase, however, further parts of the northern sector of the Reserve will be developed and opened up to tourists.

Three-quarters of the Reserve consist of dry forests, called miombo, where the dominant trees are *Brachystegia*, *Julbernardia globiflora*, *Isoberlinia*, *Pterocarpus angolensis* and *Combretum*. Other typical and easily recognizable trees are the Baobab which can live for over 2,000 years, the Sausage

Left: Elephant amongst palms

tree with its big sausage shaped fruits eaten by elephants and monkeys and the Tamarind, Mahogany, African Blackwood (*Dalbergia melanoxion*), Monkey Orange and Ebony (*Diospyros mespiliformis*), to mention just a few. The east of the Reserve is mainly grassy woodland with Terminalia species. The tourist sector north of the Rufiji River contains the whole range of vegetation to be found in the ecosystem. Miombo woodland covers the ridges of the mountains around Beho Beho and Stiegler's Gorge. There are also open woodlands with *Terminalia spinosa* trees, hardpan and short grassy plains with seasonally flooded pans. These "mbugas" or "black cotton soil" patches present an obstacle for every motorist during the rains. The savannahs provide grazing and support a wide range of wildlife, in particular wildebeest.

Impressive riverine forests and dense impenetrable thickets are important habitats of a different kind. The wide meandering Rufiji River with its associated wetlands, consisting of lakes and swamps interlaced with a myriad of channels, is one of the most outstanding ecological systems in the whole of Eastern Africa.

Characteristic Borassus palms reaching up to 25m grow in groves along the rivers. These trees need a great deal of water to survive, and can die off if the ground water level drops. The Borassus is unmistakable with its straight trunk thickening towards the top. The Doum Palm is the only multi-trunked palm which occurs. The Rufiji riverine habitat supports an abundance of wildlife such as elephants, hippos, antelopes, crocodiles and birds. The miombo woodland is adapted to long dry seasons, and its trees grow on relatively poor and infertile soils. The average rainfall in the Selous ranges from about 750mm in the east to 1300mm in the west. The rains fall from late November to May, with a drier spell during January and February.

The miombo is a woodland formation, which has been shaped over hundreds of years by annual fires either occurring naturally or lit by honey gatherers and hunters. During the dry season one gets the impression that the whole of the Selous is burning. Areas burnt early soon sprout new grass, where upon the ungulates move in. Areas burnt late may only start to regenerate in the rainy season. These annual fires also hinder tree growth, but many Miombo trees are fire resistant.

There are differing arguments as to how these fires should be viewed. Some people see them as destructive to vegetation, especially to trees and small animals, and think that all attempts should be made to extinguish the fires. Others argue that bushfires are bound to happen and are an integral part of the ecosystem. For that reason fires are started by the administration itself, because it is considered better to have an early season "cold" fire, which is not so destructive as a late season "hot" fire when temperatures are higher and the grass drier.

An important inhabitant of the miombo woodlands is the tsetse fly. Although harmless to wildlife it carries a deadly disease for domestic livestock. The fly has discouraged human settlements and livestock in the Reserve. Some conservationists say therefore that the tsetse fly is the most effective game guard. The fly can transmit sleeping sickness to humans, but no cases have been known in the Selous area for decades.

Left: Old buffalo bulls abound
Next page: One of the many crocodiles in the Rufiji River

WILDLIFE OF THE SELOUS

Moving on Hooves - The Ungulates

The Selous Game Reserve is home to the largest buffalo population in Africa. According to counts the Reserve's population stands at between 110,000 and 160,000, more than double the population of all countries in Southern Africa together. To see a herd of several hundred buffalo coming to drink at the Rufiji River in the late afternoon hours is a scene never to be forgotten. The biggest concentration we have observed counted around 3,000 animals, but this is rather rare. Herds look rather chaotic and disorderly but in reality they have a coherent social organisation. Individual buffaloes tend to keep the same location within the herd. Dominant animals stay at the front of the herd and therefore have better access to food. These are usually the larger animals or cows with calves. The animals at the rear consequently are in a poorer physical condition. While she is breeding, a female might improve her location, but may then have to return to the rear after weaning her calf.

Left: Staying cool from the heat of the day - buffalo bull

A large herd offers the best protection against predators. Solitary or small groups of bulls run a higher risk of attack from lions. Old bulls normally stay with the herd only temporarily during breeding as they quickly lose condition when mating and fighting with other males. They will leave the herd to regain weight and improve their condition again before rejoining.

Both sexes carry horns and sometimes those of the females are wider than those of the males. However as female horns are usually slimmer and the "boss" not so pronounced, they can easily be differentiated from the males. Buffalo feed mainly on grass but as they have the most efficient digestive system of all the East African herbivores they are adaptable and can also subsist on fibrous plants which other grazers cannot process. Lions are their main enemies. Many stories are told about their alleged ferocity, but like all animals they tend to avoid humans unless they are harassed or wounded.

Before the beginning of the 20th century the buffalo nearly died out due to an epidemic of rinderpest which was transmitted from domestic cattle brought to Eritrea by the Italians for their Ethiopia campaign. The epidemic swept through the whole of Africa from North to South and decimat-

ed buffaloes and antelopes.

The Selous wildebeest has a greyish-yellowish body colour, a black beard and tail, and is also known as Nyasaland gnu. As the name suggests, it was formerly found in Nyasaland (now Malawi), up to Mozambique and Southern Tanzania. Now the Selous Game Reserve is its last stronghold. It is clearly differentiated by size and colouration from the other wildebeest subspecies. It has a distinctive white, inverted chevron across the nose. Interestingly enough, south of the Rufiji River nearly all wildebeest carry this stripe. North of the river, in the tourist areas, only a few (around 1%) carry the stripe, although they are all the same subspecies.

Lichtenstein's hartebeest is one of the recognized eight subspecies. Their horns are clearly different to those of their relatives of Northern Tanzania, so they are easily identifiable. The horns are relatively thick at the base, strongly ringed, except at the tips, and Z-shaped. Both sexes carry horns, and young males and older females are difficult to differentiate. The rather awkward typical "kongoni" body form with the shoulders higher than the rump and the limp-like slow running mode is typical for all the different subspecies. Lichtenstein's are miombo animals, but they can also be found on the plains along the road towards Kinyanguru. They are grazers and usually live in small herds of up to fifteen animals.

The most common of all the antelopes is the impala, a graceful animal of medium size. They occur in either small bachelor herds or in breeding herds consisting of one adult male and many females with young. In the Community Wildlife Management Area north of the Mgeta River (which some politicians want to flood through the Kidunda dam), just before the rains start, pure male herds of up to 1,000 animals can be found, an unbelievable sight unrivalled anywhere in the world. Impala are active throughout the day and are tremendous jumpers, especially if frightened.

Impala will graze and browse and can utilise a wide variety of habitats. Consequently, even dry areas can support large numbers. When disturbed, the males emit short snorts before they take off in a wonderful spectacle of leaps and bounds. Mixed herds of impala, wildebeest, zebra and even hartebeest are a common sight. The senses of the different animals complement each other. They are safer when they move together.

Left: One of an estimated 40,000 hippos living in the Selous

The greater kudu is a spectacular and unmistakable large antelope which is not seen so often. It has long ears, slightly humped shoulders and eight to ten white vertical stripes on the body. How difficult it may be to find them can be looked up in Hemingway's "Green Hills of Africa". Kudus occur in small herds, but the adult bulls, with their distinctive long spiralled horns, are often solitary. They are well camouflaged and sharp eyes are needed to spot this greyish-brown antelope resting in the shadow of a bush, protecting itself from the heat of the day. The best chance to come across them is the bush land between Mtemere and Mbuyu, in particular where the road passes Lake Nzerakela or on the first part of the road towards Kinyanguru and West of this area.

The Selous ecosystem is one of the strongholds of sable antelope. The Reserve itself has not less than 4,000 and in the buffer zones, in particular in the south and in the northwest of the Reserve, there might be another 6,000 or so. However, in the tourist sector they are rather rare and observations are not common. They do not occur at all around the lakes and the Rufiji. Regard yourself lucky if you spot them on the road between Kisaki village and Matambwe and also along the road from Matambwe up to Stiegler's Gorge.

The Selous sable do not differ much in size from the other sable in central and Western Tanzania, and perhaps being slightly lighter in colour. However, they have generally shorter horns. Whereas the horns of bulls of the common sable (*H.h.kirkii*) easily measure more than 40 inches, this is very rare for a sable in the Selous. Here the average is about 10% less.

Both sexes have horns. Those of the male turn black when they get older. Young and female animals are brownish, but old females can also be rather dark. Recent genetic research by the Selous Conservation Programme and GTZ has discovered that the Selous sable are of the subspecies *Roosevelti*, which are regarded as highly endangered, because only about 100 have survived in the Kenyan Shimba Hills Nature Reserve, the only other remaining range. The southern limit is the Ruvuma and Niassa according to our research.

The eland is also commonly seen in the Selous. It is the largest of all the antelopes with adult bulls weighing up to 800kg. Despite their size and weight they are magnificent jumpers, leaping more than two metres even from a

Top: A mixed herd of Nyasa wildebeest and zebra

standing position. They are gregarious creatures, moving around in herds of sometimes up to a hundred animals. Bulls are more dark - greyish in colour, particularly when they get older. They are also more massive in size with thicker horns than the females. The most numerous herds of eland occur in the open plains towards Kinyanguru. The Selous eland bulls are known for their horn sizes, the largest of all East African eland. They have increased in number in the last 15 years and are now a common sight in the most northern parts of the Reserve.

Eastern Bohor reedbuck can also be seen in the same area. They are slightly smaller than impala and reddish in colour. Only the males have horns, which are ringed and curve forward. Their preferred habitat is in reed beds near swamps where they may occur in high densities.

The visitor with good eyesight and patience, or even just pure luck, might be able to see the bushbuck. They are quite common but are mainly nocturnal. During daytime they hide in dense bush land alongside rivers and lakes, but often take a stroll at midday. Their colour is reddish brown with vertical white bands and white spots on the flanks. They emit a loud alarm bark and live either singly or, in case of females with offspring or sub adults, in pairs or small groups. The males have vertical twisted horns. Should you see a brown medium-sized antelope suddenly leap out of long grass and immediately disappear into the next thicket, it is most likely a bushbuck.

The common waterbuck occurs in large numbers along the Rufiji River and around the lakes. It is a large plump animal somewhat resembling the red deer of Europe. A broad white ring encircles the rump, and this is the major visual difference to the other subspecies, the defassa waterbuck. The smallest of the antelope family, also occur – the common bush duiker, the red duiker (Harveys) and the tiny suni.

Zebras are common everywhere and the Rufiji River is the southern limit of the range of the giraffe in East Africa. There are no giraffes to be found in the southern parts of the Reserve. Brian Nicholson, the former Chief Warden, estimated their number as less than a hundred in the early seventies, but today they are plentiful. As a national symbol, they are not hunted legally anywhere in Tanzania.

Warthogs are diurnal animals and are commonly seen running for cover with their tails up, or kneeling on their front legs while feeding on short grass, roots and fruits. Some people say they are so ugly that they are almost beautiful! Their eyesight is poor, so when approached they will often advance towards the observer, but scent and hearing are well developed. They require water daily and so never move far away from it and often spend the night in abandoned aardvark holes. With a little experience it is possible for the visitor to differentiate between the males and the females, as the latter do not develop the prominent upper warts below eyes. Old males can grow enormous tusks, which are used as formidable weapons against predators.

Bush pigs on the other hand are rarely seen because they are mainly nocturnal and prefer to rest during the day in dense thickets close to rivers or wet areas. Individuals can weigh up to 80kg. They are brownish in colour, with white markings on the head and a white mane down the back. They resemble the European wild boar. Visitors may see them if driving very early in the morning close to the Rufiji River. As with all pigs, they feed on anything they find, such as roots, wild fruits, eggs, insects or meat.

Left: Young impala ewe

The Pachyderms

The Selous Game Reserve is famous for its elephant population. Unfortunately, due to heavy and continuous commercial poaching up until the early 1990's, the elephant population had been decimated from an estimated 110,000 animals in the mid seventies to less than 30,000 in 1989. Successful conservation measures have since then led to an increase of well over 60,000. More than half of Tanzania's elephants occur in the Selous. Where else should they survive, if not here?

In the Selous Game Reserve, elephants are seldom seen in large herds but more often live in small family groups led by a matriarch. Bull elephants prefer to stay in the denser thickets but will from time to time associate with the family herds.

Intensive pressure from poaching during the eighties resulted in fewer elephants with large tusks, fewer bull herds and an unbalanced age structure. The elephant population has greatly recovered during the last decade. Their impact upon the vegetation has become clearly visible, and in populated areas around the Reserve damage to cultivation is on the increase. Bulls with tusks weighing 80 pounds or more per tusk are known to exist, but are still very unlikely to be seen. However, since poaching was stopped, quite a number of bulls have grown into the 50 to 70 pound class. They are quite an impressive sight. A good place to find these is around Beho Beho towards Lake Tagalala.

Elephants shape the environment they live in. The miombo woodlands normally host few animals, but when elephants move through, branches are broken, trees are pulled down and temporary spaces are created, providing forage for a greater variety of mixed feeders, which in turn sustain an abundance of carnivores. So what looks at first sight like destructive elephant behaviour is actually the creation of a mosaic of vegetation in various stages of regeneration. The elephant is one of the architects of the miombo woodlands and savannahs of the Selous, and if the species is exterminated, the vegetation will change and other species will suffer.

Although elephants are peaceful animals they should be treated with caution and should not be approached too closely. If a young bull or a matriarch flaps its ears, raises its trunk and advances forwards, this is usually just a mock charge to scare away an intruder. It takes nerves to face a mock charge and only an experienced game

Left: Elephant bull in threatening pose

scout can tell whether the animal really means business. It is far better for the visitor not to take chances.

The black rhino population in the Selous has been affected by poaching more than any other species. The name "black rhino" is misleading, as it is no blacker than the white rhino is white. It has a hooked upper lip that enables it to browse (eat leaves) and is also referred to as the prehensile- or hook-lipped rhinoceros. The white rhino is a square lipped grazer, and has never been found in Tanzania. Female rhinos are heavier than the males and can reach up to 1,300kg.

Black rhinos are usually solitary unlike their "white" relatives. The horn is not a true horn but is made of thickly matted hair, lacking a bony core. The horn will grow again if it breaks off. Dehorning was actually proposed as a way to protect rhinos from poachers. The horn is their dilemma and the reason why they have been poached to near extinction. In Asia, rhinoceros horn is always in demand for use in traditional medicine and it is still used to treat all kinds of different ailments from colds to heart disease. However, it is rarely used as an aphrodisiac as is widely believed. Most of horn went to the North Yemen where it was used for dagger handles. This serves no other purpose but to show that the owner is sufficiently wealthy and can afford it. All trade in rhino products has been banned under the Convention on the International Trade in Endangered Species (CITES) since 1973. Unfortunately the high price paid for the horn serves as a powerful incentive to poachers and the ban has not saved the rhinos from near extinction.

In the early eighties the population in the Selous was estimated at around 3,000 rhinos. This was the largest population in Africa and the short-sighted and occasionally ill tempered heavyweights were a common sight everywhere. Now there are only a few scattered populations remaining, which hide in the dense thickets.

Efforts by the Selous administration in cooperation with the Selous Rhino Trust, the European Union and GTZ have led to a slow recovery of the rhino population. Ninteen animals are known to live in the north. Starting from a nucleus area where a few had survived they have spread into the northern sector. Tracks are easier to find and sightings are possible again. Such sightings should be reported and if possible, photographs should be taken. Photos allow identification of individual animals and they enable the Selous administration to build up a database of the population. This is usually done using the horn structure and the notches and cuts in the ears of the animals, which are characteristic to an individual.

Another interesting method of identifying individuals is through the DNA-analysis of droppings. Dung normally has some organic matter attached to it, which allows genetic "fingerprinting" unless it is too dry. Then the dung can be linked to specific animals. This is, however, technically complicated and is not always reliable.

What is the future of the black rhino in the Selous? In the early nineties the relentless persecution stopped and a remnant of the former population has survived the slaughter. Individual beasts are getting more relaxed and are even seen in the open during daytime. There are sightings of calves and youngsters now and younger males have been seen wandering about far away from their home range. There has been no signs of poaching in the last 15 years. All this makes us moderately optimistic about the long-term survival of the species in the Reserve.

Another heavyweight, the hippopotamus, lives in high densities

---

Left: Rhino near Beho Beho River

in the rivers and lakes of the Selous. There are now some 40,000 hippos in the Selous. This number is probably higher than the carrying capacity of the Reserve and die offs at the end of the dry season due to lack of food are not uncommon. During the daytime they prefer to stay in the water, but at night they come ashore and wander inland to graze. They can also be found in very small creeks and even in isolated water holes far away from the rivers. Hippos must keep their 5 cm thick skin moist and, if away from water, they secrete the equivalent of a sun screen lotion, which is reddish in colour.

Hippos can remain submerged for up to five minutes. Schools of hippo can be quite aggressive in the water, but their awkward lunging movements towards a boat will normally be only a mock charge. In a real attack they move just under the surface of the water and try to upset the boat from underneath. The bulls fight each other quite frequently and it is a common sight to see hippos with scars and even with severe wounds.

Teeth and Claws - the Predators

The Selous has a healthy population of 3,000 to 4,000 lions. They are a common sight everywhere in the northern sector of the Selous, in particular along the lakes and in the Beho Beho area. Due to the dense vegetation they are, however, less frequently observed compared to the open grasslands of Ngorongoro and the Serengeti. According to research 11 prides with about 80 adults and over 20 cubs live along the Rufiji River. Such figures will vary, however, considerably over time.

The distant roaring of lions, which can be heard as far as 8km, is a common sound at night and is rather frightening, if you are lying in a tent and can hear the lions coming closer. Contrary to common belief lions are not afraid of open fires and when fly camping in the bush, visitors are recommended not to wander around in the darkness. A tent is, however, perfectly safe even if a whole pride decides to settle in front of it.

Some animals such as snakes and crocodiles have a bad image because of evil connotations, but lions are regarded as a symbol of majesty - the king of the beasts, the master of the animal kingdom. In reality, lions do not live up to human expectations. They simply behave like lions. If given the chance, they will steal the prey of other carnivores rather than hunt for themselves. The females do most of the hunting, but the males will take over the prey and fill their stomachs first. Young lions are the last in the hierarchy to feed from a carcass and when prey animals are scarce, cubs may starve because the older ones including their mothers leave them nothing to eat. Cubs can also die because they are deserted by their mothers or killed by males who have recently taken over the pride. Occasionally hye-

Top: Lion cub relaxing in a tree

nas will kill a lion cub, but otherwise they have no natural enemies apart from man.

Many attacks on prey animals, which can be anything from an impala to a buffalo, are unsuccessful. When lions do succeed in catching a larger animal they pull their victim down, bite into the throat and slowly strangle it.

A pride of lions consists of females and their cubs with the male lions joining a family for several months or years, until other males force them out. Fights between male lions are common, often leading to the death of the loser.

Lions are less popular with the people living around the Selous than they are with tourists. In some years up to 50 villagers were killed by lions in the vicinity of the Reserve, not to mention the loss of life through crocodiles, elephants and hippos. Between August 2003 and April 2004 a total of 35 humans were killed and a

© Pietro Luraschi

similar number badly mauled by one single male lion in the fields south of the Rufiji, near the entrance to the Reserve at Mtemere. This simba, nicknamed 'Ossama' by the local people, specialized in jumping on the straw roofs of huts and then falling through onto the sleeping inhabitants. Most of the temporary homesteads between the south shore of the river and the reserve boundary were consequently deserted and the fertile fields were slowly returning to bush, leaving the farmers to go hungry. The area is very wild with dense vegetation and the scouts had failed to hunt this maneater down. One night this lion attacked a fisherman on an island and then swam to the northern shore. It was at last shot there by game rangers after a driven hunt with hundreds of villagers, but only after it had killed three more women. The lion was a fat male in its prime which would have been well able to feed on the buffaloes, antelopes and bushpigs in his home range. However, it suffered from a broken molar and an abscess and consequently from a bad toothache. In Tanzania as a whole 200 or more human deaths result from wild animals annually, more proof of the great sacrifice made by the country in the name of conservation. Fortunately no casualties have occurred amongst tourists in the Selous, but utmost care is advised with all dangerous game, in particular if the visitor is on foot.

Leopards are seldom seen as they are mainly nocturnal and it is therefore commonly assumed that the leopard is a much rarer species. This is not at all the case in the Selous and its surroundings. In fact, they by far outnumber the

Left: Crocodiles measuring up to 5m have been found in the Reserve

© Pietro Luraschi

lions. Leopards are solitary creatures and visitors may consider themselves very lucky to see one. As it is no longer fashionable to wear spotted furs, killing leopards for their skins is now rare and it is no longer an endangered species.

Leopards are well adapted to many of Selous' habitats but prefer dense bush and thickets. They can live in close proximity to humans and occasionally catch chickens at Matambwe game post. Being very efficient hunters leopards can kill any mammal up to the size of a bushbuck. Although they also like to eat fish, insects and birds, monkeys are one of their favourite foods. Often they will haul their kill up into the branches of a tree and return for feeding. Scratches in the bark show the attentive eye that leopards are around. Leopards are dangerous animals and although attacks on humans are rare, they nevertheless

occur. An unusual incident happened in March 2004 when a leopard killed a man returning from his field in a village south of the Reserve. Then a lion appeared, chased away the leopard and ate the poor victim.

The cheetah also occurs in the Northern and Eastern Selous. It has always been extremely rare, but several sightings have been confirmed in recent years. A cheetah has even been photographed at Kinyanguru. We would be delighted to receive further photos, if visitors are so lucky as to see one of these elegant felines. It is probable that the Miombo woodlands of the Selous are not very suitable for the cheetah. They also suffer from the high density of other predators and the resulting competition. The same might be true for black-backed and side-striped jackals, both of which occur, but not in large numbers. South of the Rufiji they are more common.

The African wild dog is disappearing throughout Africa, although it is a protected species. It is estimated that only 3,000 to 4,000 are left. Its natural habitats are being destroyed for cultivation and livestock owners persecute the dogs which are easy to kill. It is nearly extinct now in the Serengeti, probably due to strong competition from spotted hyenas and lions, which are both very common there, and due to diseases transmitted by the domestic dogs of herdsmen. In hot and emotional debates between different camps of researchers it was also questioned whether even the research work on wild dogs has played a role in the extinction. The controversy could never be solved scientifically, both parties having arguments in their favour.

Left: Leopard relaxing in a tree

On the other hand the Selous dogs are thriving. According to a conservative estimate by researchers who have studied them for five years, there are approximately 1,300 wild dogs in the Reserve, including pups. Of these, about 900 are adults and yearlings. However, additional dogs live in the ecosystem, for example another 140 in Mikumi and unknown numbers in the community wildlife management areas around the Reserve. The entire population might thus make up more than half of the continental figure. It is without doubt the largest and most important on the whole continent, and the Selous is the only place where a visitor has a reasonable chance of observing wild dogs. If found, they do not show fright and it is often possible to observe their intense social life at close quarters. In the tourist areas the density of dogs is 1 dog per 17km^2 (incl. puppies) or 1 adult per 25km^2. This is higher than anywhere else in Africa. In the rest of the Selous, where the habitat and the prey availability is less favourable, the density is approx. 1 adult per 56km^2. The population peaks annually in September/October. At this time, adults comprise two thirds of the total population.

Due to their social behaviour

and their cooperative hunting in groups of 3 to 20 dogs, they are very efficient hunters. Almost every second hunting attempt is successful. This is one of the reasons for their well-being, together with the lack of human persecution. But the Selous dogs also look after themselves. They avoid lions, which kill them if given a chance. They also loose little food (2%) to spotted hyenas, unlike wild dogs in some other parks. In Serengeti, wild dogs lost up to 86% of their kills to spotted hyenas.

Wild dogs depend largely on their eyesight and hunt only in daytime. A hunt is preceded by licking and playing until the pack gets excited and a general chirping indicates that the hunt is ready to set off. They chase as a team, running their prey down and pulling it to a halt by the rump, and if it is a small animal it is devoured in a matter of moments.

Wild dogs are able to catch animals as large as wildebeest or zebras and their method of killing is for one or two members of the pack to immobilise the prey by biting into its nose and holding it firmly. The others will then kill the prey by disembowelling it. Wild dogs are not large, and they do not

Left and top: Wild dogs can catch animals as large as wildebeest

have a single "killing bite" as the big cats do, so they cannot kill large prey in any other way. Some people consider this an unpleasant scene to witness and wild dogs are often thought of as cruel. It is this typical human misunderstanding of animal behaviour which has contributed in the past to the relentless persecution of the wild dog. Up until the seventies even famous park wardens would shoot them on sight within the national parks as they were regarded as pests and seen as harmful to game. Given the fact that wild dogs are always much less abundant than spotted hyenas and lions, they would have little impact on prey populations, even if prey were limited by predation, and many prey populations are not limited by predators, but by their own food supply.

Usually only the dominant female of the pack breeds and she can give birth to up to 12 puppies. The whole pack cooperates in rearing the pups and one dog will stay behind to guard the den when the rest of the pack goes hunting. On return from the hunt food is regurgitated by the adults to feed the puppies.

The spotted hyena is mainly a nocturnal animal, but a good observer can spot them during the day resting in a bush or in a ditch. Most of the time hyenas are seen alone, but to conclude from that that they are solitary animals like leopards would be completely wrong. To the contrary, they are socially highly organised animals. The centre of their clan life is the den. A clan can consist of between 40 and 80 members. In the den the female raise the young, and it is off limits for the male hyenas. The clans have a very strict hierarchy. On the top is the alpha female, followed by her female relatives.

The highest male is lower in the hierarchy than the lowest female. Hyenas often hunt alone, up to 70km from the den depending on the availability of food. The young wait at the den for their mothers to return and feed them. If the mother is killed the young starve to death, because they are not fed by the other females.

The ancient Greeks believed, incorrectly, that hyenas were hermaphrodites, having both male and female organs. Their sexual organs look alike, and although females are larger than males, it is difficult to differentiate between them from a distance.

It is also a fallacy that the hyena eats only rotten meat or the leftovers from a lion kill. Hyenas are efficient hunters and more often than not, lions feed on their kills. Hyenas can reach a speed of up to 60km/h and can follow their

Top: Spotted hyenas are common in the Selous

prey over many kilometres. Their whooping call, which starts on a low note and ends on a high one, is a sound typical of the African night and has sent many a shiver down a visitor's spine! Sometimes one can hear almost human sounding demented laughing and cackling at night. These are hyenas feeding. The laughing is their way of dinner talk. Hyenas are common in the Selous, their population density being three times that of the lions.

Other Wildlife

The yellow baboon, the vervet, and the blue monkey are a common sight everywhere. In certain riverine forests the impressive black and white colobus can be found moving from tree to tree in family groups. They live in small territories and subsist mainly on leaves, unlike most other monkeys. If you are interested, ask your guide to take you to places where they are known to occur.

A very rare and endangered monkey, the Iringa or Uhehe red colobus lives in the Magombera forest along the Tazara Railway south of Msolwa in Western Selous. They should be mentioned as a tourist attraction, although none occur in the northern sector, the focus of this travel guide. The total number in the Selous is not more than 400 animals. This little monkey which is closely related to the Zanzibar red colobus also lives in the recently proclaimed Udzungwa National Park. Fortunately the Selous has so far been able to protect it, although its range lies mainly outside the protected area. Interested visitors may arrange a visit with the Selous management. The visitor can travel by car or train to Msolwa and camp there at the game scout station. A ranger can then take you on a one hour walk to the forest, where the monkeys can be easily observed.

Crocodiles are abundant in the

Rufiji River and all the surrounding lakes with some individuals measuring up to 5m. They are the largest reptiles in the world, and live mostly on fish but will prey upon smaller and even larger animals when these come to the river to drink. The crocodile swims as close as it can to a possible victim and the ensuing attack is powerful and fast. On land they walk with their entire body clear of the ground and can move at high speed if necessary. Many human deaths result from crocodile attacks, especially in areas where settlements are situated on the banks of large African rivers. Crocodiles have always been equated with evil and some of the early European explorers boasted in their books of shooting them by the dozens so as to relieve mankind of a pest. They are, however, social animals who care for their offspring. After laying and burying the eggs in the sand the female guards them until they are ready to hatch. She then excavates the hatchlings and carries them in her mouth to the water where they

Top: A crocodile contemplating its next meal

are watched over for up to three months. The same jaws that can twist the hind leg off a buffalo carcass can carry a tiny soft baby crocodile without so much as a scratch. However, these same crocodiles are responsible for much loss of human life and injuries in the Ruvu and Mgeta Rivers north of the Selous.

Snakes are common everywhere and one of the "fathers" of the Reserve, Constantine Ionides, was given the nickname "Snake Man" due to his hobby of catching and keeping poisonous green and black mambas, puff adders, spitting cobras and gaboon vipers. Most snakes you might encounter are harmless, and they will all do everything possible to avoid you. Snake bites are, therefore, extremely rare.

The most common fish in the Rufiji and the lake systems are different types of catfish, especially the sharp and blunt toothed varieties. The latter can grow to an enormous size and individuals of up to 40kg have been caught. Tigerfish are also common. For sports fishermen it is one of the most sought after gamefish, due to its habit of fighting hard and jumping frequently when caught on a line. More often than not they

are able to get rid of the hook in the process. A rare visitor to the Rufiji is the bull or Zambezi shark. Small young sharks have been caught occasionally. This remarkable shark is able to live in fresh water for extended periods, and it enters the Rufiji delta and swims up the river as far as Kibambawe which is a distance from the sea of not less than 200km. The robust bodied shark attains a length of 320cm and can weigh over 300kg. The bull shark is a powerful and dangerous predator, capable of feeding in dirty water and is one of the most dangerous sharks to humans.

The fishing villages along the Rufiji were removed prior to the seventies to give space to the Reserve, but the descendants of the former inhabitants still enter the Reserve with their dugout canoes at night and fish illegally, as the waters are so rich in fish. The tourist camps on the Rufiji have fishing tackle available for the visitor, and so far the Reserve has not charged a fee for fishing.

Left: Hooded and Griffon Vultures
Right: Monitor Lizard
Next page: River scene

A BIRDERS' PARADISE

Although Selous is best known for the spectacular large mammals set in this vast area of wilderness, visitors cannot fail to notice its abundant and varied bird life. More than 440 species have been recorded in Selous and an up-to-date bird list can be obtained at the tourist camps. The following account describes where to find some of the more conspicuous and noteworthy species.

Birds of the Wetlands

One of the best ways to see water birds on the constantly changing pattern of sandbanks, oxbow lakes, lagoons, islands and channels along the Rufiji River, is to take the river trip offered by many of the lodges. The African Skimmer is most eye-catching as it flies close to the surface of the water, dipping the tip of its elongated lower bill, and snapping its beak closed when it touches a fish. The statuesque Goliath Heron and Saddle-billed Stork are often spotted fishing alone in the shallows. At times, flocks of hundreds of Open-billed and Yellow-billed Storks can be seen wheel-

Top: Lilac-breasted Roller

ing over the wetlands while riverbanks may reveal nesting burrows of bee-eaters such as the White-fronted Bee-eater or a variety of kingfishers, sometimes with their owners in attendance. Of the ten species of kingfisher found in Selous, the Pied Kingfisher is an ever-present black and white member of the wetland community, which uniquely amongst its relatives, hovers over the water before plunging to catch fish. The Half-collared and Giant Kingfishers are less common and fish from perches by the wooded riverbanks. The African Fish Eagle whose yelping call is one of Africa's most distinctive sounds, preys on fish although it may occasionally take the young of Egyptian Geese.

The scenery of the Rufiji River is made all the more spectacular by the groves of Borassus Palms. The slender Palm Swift, in a remarkable departure from the nesting habits of most birds, glues its eggs to the underside of palm leaves with its own adhesive saliva. Dead, hollow, leafless trunks provide vantage points for birds of prey such as the Red-necked Falcon and nesting sites for Egyptian Geese and Dickinson's Kestrels.

Lakes such as Nzerakela and Tagalala are excellent places to watch a fantastic variety of water birds attracted to the fish and other aquatic life, which become concentrated as the water levels fall during the dry season. Great White Pelicans fish in coordinated groups, each dipping its great head and bill into the water in unison, while the more common Pink-backed Pelican fishes alone. Also seen on or around the water are Little Grebes, Long-tailed Cormorant and Greater Cormorants as well as a variety of geese and ducks such as the Pygmy Goose, White-faced Whistling Ducks,

White-backed Duck and Red-billed Teal. In the shallows Little Egret, Yellow-billed Egret and Madagascar Squacco Herons can be found along with a vast array of waders including Black-winged Stilts, sandpipers and plovers.

Sandbanks are the haunts of resting Skimmers, terns (eg White-winged Black Tern and Whiskered Tern) and the White-headed Lapwing the last being an unusual and local species for which the Rufiji River and its tributaries are a major stronghold. At times lapwings incubating eggs or guarding their downy chicks are conspicuous on the sandbanks. A much sharper eye is required to see the diminutive White-fronted Plover, which blends with the sand. Visitors to Stiegler's Gorge who scan the rocks carefully might be lucky to find the White-collared Pratincole which is a very rare bird of fast-flowing rocky sections of the river.

In heavily wooded sections of the riverbank the Pel's Fishing Owl spends its daylight hours in large riverine trees but may sometimes be seen fishing over the river and lagoons at dawn or dusk. Its call is an unmistakable spine-chilling shriek. The White-backed Night Heron is another elusive nocturnal species of wooded river banks and oxbows.

Some other good sightings in the wetlands include: Darter, Little and Dwarf Bittern. Purple and Rufous Bellied Heron, Osprey, Corncrake, African and Black Crake, Finfoot, Painted Snipe, Kittlitz's Plover, Whiskered and White-winged Black Tern.

Right: Weaver bird
Top: Pied Kingfisher

... of the Woodlands

Miombo woodland dominates the Selous ecosystem and is home to a variety of colourful and interesting birds. Insectivorous species abound and may include such notables as Thick-billed Cuckoo, Bohm's Bee-eater, Raquet-tailed Roller, Pale-billed Hornbills, Red-throated Wryneck, and Stierling's Woodpecker. Mixed species flocks of woodland birds (also known as bird parties) can be found travelling and feeding together and offer the observer an opportunity to stay still and let many species pass close-by in a short space of time. Common Scimitarbill, Klaas's Cuckoo, Olive Woodpecker, Green Tinkerbird, Green-capped Eremomela and Brubru are commonly found in such flocks.

Attracting attention with their loud screeching calls, parrots whiz overhead in a greenish blur. The Brown-necked Parrot is uncommon in East Africa but can be found in the wooded hills above Beho Beho. Associated with baobab trees, occasionally large flocks gather at water holes or fruiting trees. The smaller Brown-headed Parrot is much more common.

In the woodlands also look out for: Whyte's Barbet, Miombo Rock Thrush, Green-capped Eremomela and Barred Wren-warbler.

... of the Forests

In certain localities in Selous such as along riverbanks, woodlands can often give way to forest. Forest birding is always challeng-

ing and many birds may be heard but not seen, but the best time to find birds is early morning and evening. Among the varied bird life of this dense riverine habitat is a southern speciality, the Livingstone's Flycatcher. Bright yellow below and with a chestnut tail, Selous is its stronghold in Tanzania. The striking Dark-backed Weaver is another forest species which is easily seen and their long-spouted woven nests are evident over drainage lines. Livingstone's and Violet-crested Turacos are two examples of a spectacular group of birds only found in Africa and are most often seen when a short glide from one tree to another exposes their brilliant red wings. The curious sound of the African Broadbill produced by air moving through stiff wing feathers, is often heard in these forests, but a sighting of the small brown bird usually requires careful and patient stalking. The lucky observer will see the Broadbill make a short circular display flight and return to its perch, while exposing the white feathers of its back. The forest floor is the home of the Kenya Crested Guinea fowl which, like its helmeted cousin in the woodlands, lives in flocks. The largest avian predator of the forest is the Crowned Eagle, a bird powerful enough to hunt monkeys and small antelopes. It may sometimes be seen flying high above the forest in its tumbling aerial display while uttering a far-carrying, undulating shrill call. With persistence,

Left: Brown-hooded Kingfisher
Top: Grey Heron

species such as the Four-coloured Bush-shrike, Square-tailed Drongo, Narina Trogon, Barred Long-tailed Cuckoo, Yellowbill and many others may be seen in the forests of the Selous.

... of the Grasslands

The grasslands of Selous are typically spotted with Terminalia and Acacia trees. No less than 56 birds of prey and vultures have been found throughout the ecosystem although they may be most frequently spotted in these lightly wooded grasslands. If you gaze up at the sky, it will not be long before a Bateleur soars into view. Although it preys on snakes, birds and small mammals, it may also eat carrion. This species is well known for its exceptional eyesight and a Bateleur diving earthwards is the signal for any vulture within sight to follow in the hopes of sharing the food. White-backed Vultures and Hooded Vultures are the common species in Selous and a congregation may indicate a predator's kill. Look out also for the more solitary Lappet-faced Vultures and White-headed Vultures, and those rare nomads from the grasslands of Northern Tanzania, the Rüppell's Griffon and Egyptian Vultures. The Shikra is the most frequently seen small hawk while the huge Martial Eagle may be seen hunting large birds and even medium sized mammals. Some species, such as the Hobby, Eleanora's Falcon, Honey Buzzard and the globally threatened Lesser Kestrel are Eurasian migrants which spend the northern winter in the tropics.

During the rainy season winged termites spread out in their millions from underground homes throughout the Selous. These insects are a major source of food for birds such as bee-eaters but they also attract the birds of prey. While Sooty Falcons catch them on the wing, the larger birds of prey such as Tawny Eagles and Steppe Eagles take them from the ground. It is comical to see these powerful predators running about pecking up the termites like chickens.

Other notable birds of prey include the Southern Banded Snake-eagle, African Cuckoo Hawk and Ayres Hawk Eagle.

Large birds such as Secretary Birds and Black-bellied and Buff-crested Bustards stalk through the grass in search of small animals. Southern Ground Hornbills live in family groups in which a breeding pair and their progeny of previous years cooperate to raise the latest hatchlings. Their deep booming calls are one of the never-to-be-forgotten sounds of the African dawn.

Helmeted Guinea Fowl, Shelley's Francolin, Red-necked Spurfowl and Blue Quail are examples of grassland birds which forage on the ground for seeds and insects. Of the many species of small birds in the grasslands, some of the more conspicuous are the weavers, sparrows and finches which congregate to drink at water holes during the dry season. The White-browed Sparrow Weaver is particularly abundant, nesting colonially in trees where it builds its untidy grass nests. The nests of this and other weavers are often raided for nestlings during the day-time by predators like the Harrier Hawk and at night by Barn Owls. Small grassland notables include: Parasitic Weaver, Olive-headed Golden Weaver, Lavender Waxbill, Orange-winged Pytilia, Broad-tailed Paradise Whydah and Stripe-breasted Seedeater.

Visitors to Selous during the dry season may encounter grass fires, often deliberately lit for management purposes. Certain birds such as Temmink's Courser are quick to assemble at the fire front to catch insects, reptiles and other small animals driven by the flames, or search the ash for those that were not quick enough to escape. Rollers, beeeaters, birds of prey, drongos, and various swallows and hornbills often attend, and the sight of smoke will bring Marabou Storks from many miles. A rare visitor from Southern Africa, the Dusky Lark, has also been recorded on recently burnt ground in

Left: Flying Ibis

Selous. The dainty Senegal Plover benefits later by laying its speckled eggs on burnt grassland where they are camouflaged from predators.

Interesting Relationships

Reminding us that birds are only a part of the larger ecosystem of the Selous, there are many examples of birds interacting with other animals which share the same habitat. A number of birds have mutually beneficial relationships with large mammals. Cattle Egrets, Northern Carmine Bee-eaters and Drongos habitually follow elephants, buffaloes and other herbivores in order to catch the insects that these large animals disturb. Relatives of the starlings, Red-billed Oxpeckers and Yellow-billed Oxpeckers crawl over the animals' bodies in search of parasites such as ticks and even peck at wounds in order to feed on the blood. The Southern Cordon Bleu, a tiny finch, is common in Selous. Despite its small size and vulnerability to predators, it does not attempt to hide its nest but builds it conspicuously close to the nest of a colonial wasp with a fierce sting. A predator intending to rob the Cordon Bleu's nest must first run the gauntlet of the

wasps protecting their own nest.

A most intimate and fascinating association is that between the Greater Honeyguide and the Honey Badger or Ratel. The honeyguide is said to lead the badger to bees' nests which the badger then raids, exposing the bees' larvae and beeswax which the bird can then eat. Curiously, in the honeyguide's stomach live microbes which can digest the otherwise indigestible wax. You would be exceptionally lucky to see this association between badger and bird in action, but the honeyguide will also guide humans to a beehive with its rattling call. The strange twists to the Greater Honeyguide's life do not end there for it does not attend to its own eggs and young. Instead, it is a brood parasite laying each egg, cuckoo-like, in the nest hole of a woodpecker or barbet. When the young hatches it kills its foster siblings and is raised to fledging by its foster parents. It is a strange sight to see a pair of Striped Kingfishers frantically feeding a young honeyguide in the mistaken belief that it is their own offspring.

Left: White-fronted Bee-eaters
Top: Egrets at Lake Tagalala
Next page: River cruise

GAME VIEWING TOURISM

The Wildlife Division of the Ministry of Natural Resources and Tourism administers the Selous Game Reserve. The headquarters is at Matambwe in the Northern Selous. A total of around 280 game scouts (approx. 1 scout per 70km^2), technical and administrative personnel are posted in the Reserve. Their main task is to patrol the area and prevent poachers from entering. They also monitor game populations and develop and maintain the necessary infrastructure such as roads, airstrips, game scout stations and outposts.

Most of these management activities are paid out of the Selous retention scheme mentioned previously. Its income is derived from two sources. The first is photographic tourism, which provides low but steady earnings. 3,500 tourists per year provide 10% of the income of the Reserve. The main income (90%), however, is derived from hunting safaris. Around 500 foreign hunters visit the southern parts of the Reserve between the months of July and November and around 3,000 animals are shot per year. This hunting is carried

Left: A dozing lioness does not mind the tourists, if they keep their distance

out on a sustainable basis, and only a fraction of the population growth is harvested. People who dislike hunting should be aware that without the income from safari hunting the Reserve could not exist.

Tourist and hunting blocks are separated from each other, and it is not possible for photographic tourists to visit the areas south of the Rufiji.

The Management Plan sets out certain policies and restrictions for the Selous. The principle is to keep human impact as low as possible, whether from the local population or from tourism. Visitors should be able to enjoy a unique and unspoiled wilderness. Photographic tourism has slowly expanded and in 2005 there are seven camps and lodges inside the Reserve (Note: Mbuyu Camp and Tembo Camp are presently not operating), with one more camp just outside the Mtemere Gate and a lodge along the Matambwe-Kisaki northern entry road.

Left: Borassus palm
Top: Zebra in lake-shore palm vegetation
Next page: Spectacular sunset over the Selous

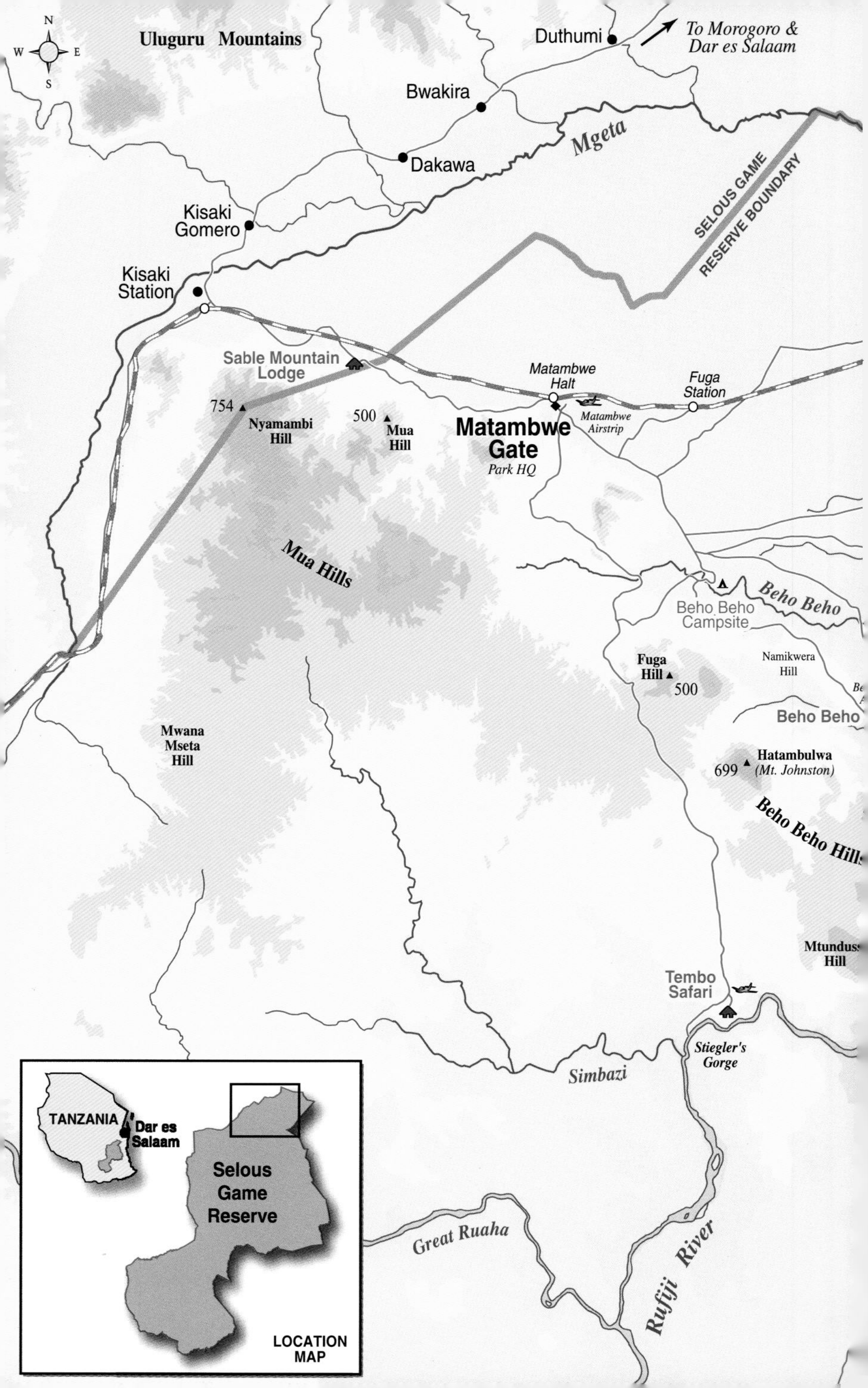
N
W
E
S
Uluguru Mountains
Duthumi
To Morogoro & Dar es Salaam
Bwakira
Mgeta
Dakawa
SELOUS GAME RESERVE BOUNDARY
Kisaki Gomero
Kisaki Station
Sable Mountain Lodge
754
Nyamambi Hill
500
Mua Hill
Matambwe Halt
Matambwe Airstrip
Matambwe Gate
Park HQ
Fuga Station
Mua Hills
Beho Beho
Beho Beho Campsite
Fuga Hill
500
Namikwera Hill
Beho Beho
Mwana Mseta Hill
Hatambulwa
699
(Mt. Johnston)
Beho Beho Hills
Mtundusi Hill
Tembo Safari
Stiegler's Gorge
Simbazi
Great Ruaha
Rufiji River
TANZANIA
Dar es Salaam
Selous Game Reserve
LOCATION MAP

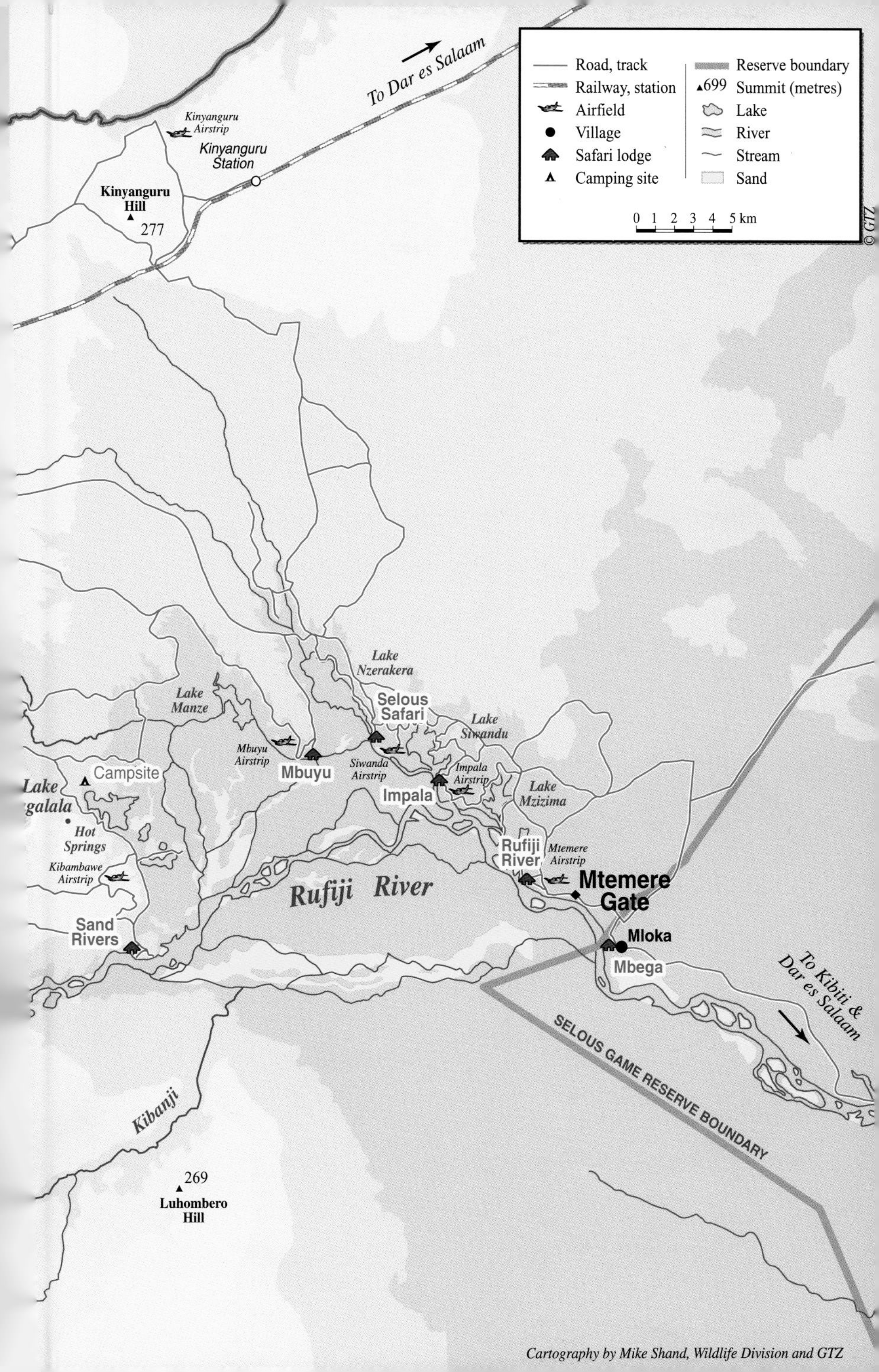

Road, track
Railway, station
Airfield
Village
Safari lodge
Camping site
Reserve boundary
699 Summit (metres)
Lake
River
Stream
Sand
0 1 2 3 4 5 km
© GTZ
To Dar es Salaam
Kinyanguru Airstrip
Kinyanguru Station
Kinyanguru Hill
277
Lake Nzerakera
Selous Safari
Lake Manze
Lake Siwandu
Mbuyu Airstrip
Mbuyu
Siwanda Airstrip
Impala Airstrip
Impala
Lake Mzizima
Campsite
Lake
galala
Hot Springs
Kibambawe Airstrip
Rufiji River
Mtemere Airstrip
Mtemere Gate
Rufiji River
Sand Rivers
Mloka
Mbega
To Kibiti & Dar es Salaam
SELOUS GAME RESERVE BOUNDARY
Kibanji
269
Luhombero Hill
Cartography by Mike Shand, Wildlife Division and GTZ

ROUTES FOR THE VISITORS AND AREAS TO SEE

Some of the main game viewing routes are described in this guide, however, there are many other additional minor tracks close to the camps.

The Main Road: Matambwe-Mtemere

During the two hour (approx. 75km) drive between the two gates, all of the typical vegetation types of the Selous can be seen as well as an impressive variety of animal species. Matambwe is situated in open woodland and after 5km on this road, a road turns off to the left, which leads to Fuga Railway Station.

After passing through some woodland, the Beho Beho Mountains come into view with their extensive Miombo cover. To reach Beho Beho, there are two turnings to the right, one at around 13km, and another at around 35km. Close to the last junction the road approaches and then follows the Rufiji River system with its lakes, streams and swamps, where herds of buffalo, impala and waterbuck graze under Borassus palms together. Elephants prefer to spend the hottest time of the

Left: Hippo

day undisturbed in the thickets towards the river. On the eastern side of the road, the undulating plains are dotted with herds of wildebeest, giraffe and the occasional elephant.

Further along, there are turnoffs leading to the tented Selous Safari Camp (56km) and to Impala Camp (60km). Here the road passes through dense bush where a variety of animals, mainly impala and zebra can be seen. Finally the Mtemere airstrip comes in sight and from here it is 2km to the right for Rufiji River Camp and a few hundred meters to the left to Mtemere gate. A German steam engine is on display there. It was manufactured in Magdeburg over one hundred years ago and could be used to run all kind of agricultural machinery. This self propelled "Dampf-Lokomobil" was taken from Kilwa by the retreating forces under von Lettow-Vorbeck in the First World War, but was soon abandoned near the Njenje River in the South-Eastern Selous from where we retrieved it.

The Rufiji River

A unique way to observe wildlife and see some of the best scenery in the Reserve is by boat on the Rufiji River. Most camps offer this facility while a cruise on Lake Tagalala is a must for visitors to Beho Beho and Sable Mountain Lodge. Private boats are not allowed. Aluminium boats with outboard engines carry passengers on the main river and the labyrinth of smaller channels, swamps and minor lakes, created by constant changes in the river course. Hippos and crocodiles are abundant, as are a large variety of water birds. Waterbuck and buffalo can be observed as they come down to drink at the river - the mock charge of a young hippo bull is a common experience. It is advisable to give these pachyderms the right of way! Fishing with a line is permitted. Ask your camp for details. You may catch tiger, catfish and squeakers and once every few years a rare visitor from the open seas, a bull shark, can be bagged.

Stiegler's Gorge with Tembo Safari Camp is about 45km from Matambwe and it takes about two hours to drive there. Immediately after Matambwe the road turns off to the right. A further 14km on, the road passes a small creek and then follows a very scenic route through hilly woodland where elephant, zebra, buffalo and eland are common. Occasionally sable antelope can be seen. Stiegler's Gorge was named after a Swiss adventurer who was killed there by an elephant around 1900, but we have not been able to find any more information on this man who gave his name to a such a conspicuous feature of the reserve. Here the Rufiji River has dug itself deep into the mountains and flows through a narrow chasm eight kilometres long. The tourist camp at Stiegler's Gorge was built in 1977, originally as a base camp for scientists and engineers who were assessing the feasibility of a dam at the gorge. Fortunately from a conservation point of view the project was abandoned. The tourist camp is presently closed. From the camp visitors have a beautiful view south over the rolling miombo woodland, which stretches as far as the eye can see. Four kilometres from the camp the abandoned dam construction site can be visited. The old and often photographed cable car over the river is still in place there and has even had test runs with passengers including our friend Benson Kibonde the Selous Warden, whose courage in using it certainly impressed us. The technical state of the cable after 25 years is doubtful, and its use for excursions to the south bank can not be recommended.

Beho Beho and Lake Tagalala

There are various routes to Beho Beho and the beautiful hinterland around Lake Tagalala. Following the Mtemere road from Matambwe there is a turn off to the right after about 12km. This road leads to a defunct bridge over the Beho Beho River, which can,

---

Left: Steam engine left behind by Lettow-Vorbeck's troops

however, be easily forded there. The road traverses hilly woodland, a favourite retreat of buffalo and elephant, until it reaches Beho Beho. At the bridge a camping site has been set up, where visitors can spend the night after first registering at Matambwe or Mtemere gate.

The shorter and better main road to Beho Beho turns off to the right shortly after the first junction. After another 11km you cross the Beho Beho River which has no water during the dry season. From the river it is another 9km to the Beho Beho Tourist Lodge which consists of bandas which were completely rebuilt in 2004. The drive from Matambwe to this camp takes a good hour.

To reach Beho Beho from Mtemere, drive along the main road for about 50km and take the turning to the left. A further 20 km across open plains where game is plentiful and Beho Beho comes into sight. This drive takes about three hours. Enquire at Mtemere Gate or at Beho Beho whether this road is passable. The Mwanamungu crossing can pose a problem. Otherwise drive on the main road towards Matambwe for approximately 63km until you see the Beho Beho signboard where you turn to the left.

The Beho Beho area experienced some fighting between English and German troops in the First World War. A short distance south-east of the airstrip are a number of trenches, now barely visible, where only a few years ago you might still have found bullets, shells and ammunition boxes.

It was here that Frederick C. Selous was killed. His grave can be found by following the road from Beho Beho back towards Matambwe. Two kilometres after passing the airstrip, the road towards Mbuyu and Mtemere branches off to the right. After another kilometre a track branches off to the right. The grave was originally marked by a simple cement plaque, which had, however, become almost illegible. When we renovated the grave in the late eighties we replaced it with an identical brass plate which reads:

Captain F.C. Selous D.S.O.
25th Royal Fusiliers
Killed in Action 4.1.1917

On the southern edge of the airstrip the road towards Lake Tagalala commences. This road is about 14km long and it takes approximately 45 minutes to reach the lake. Game is plentiful all along the way, in particular zebra and wildebeest. Buffalo can almost always be seen here, but mainly as small groups of bulls. The big herds of buffaloes usually stay in the palm swamps near the Rufiji

River. The area is also known for its lions. Lake Tagalala, like all the lakes in the area, is connected to the Rufiji River system and its size and shape is constantly changing. It is particularly renowned for its large crocodile population.

A turning off to the right here leads to the Hot Springs about 1km away which are hidden in a ravine surrounded by lush vegetation. Hot sulphurous water flows from the rocks, and pours down the mountain in small streams which finally join together in a series of picturesque pools. They used to be shadowed by lush tropical vegetation, but the increasing elephant population has decimated the trees and bushes which once hid and overgrew the Hot Springs.

From Lake Tagalala the road leads southwards to Sand Rivers Selous. The distance between Matambwe and this lodge is just under 50km.

A New Tourist Zone: Kinyanguru

The Kinyanguru area in the extreme north-eastern edge of the Reserve used to be a hunting block. In accordance with the Management Plan it has been earmarked now for photographic tourism, although this will be a financial loss to the Reserve. When travelling from Mbuyu Camp towards Mtemere there is a road turning to the left which leads in the direction of Kinyanguru Hill.

Top: The many lakes invite boat trips

The unmistakable little mountain with an elevation of around 300m height is surrounded by low-lying country and gave the area its name. While walking up to the top the hiker will meet herds of buffaloes, the unavoidable wildebeest and has a good chance of running into elephants. In the last few years you might even have been lucky enough to see an impressive old tusker, as they seem to like hanging around here – a sight which was unthinkable in the nineties. The prominent hill lies not more than 5km south of the Mgeta River which is the Reserve's northern edge. The Tazara railway crosses the area and Kinyanguru station is not far. This station serves no purpose apart from servicing needs of the trains, and it is said that the Chinese railway engineers simply followed their home pattern and built a station every 30km. Visitors to the Selous can get off the train only if a pickup has been arranged in advance with one of the camps, as there is otherwise no transport. The Tazara railway is built along the watershed between the Ruvu and Rufiji Rivers, which is a low and hardly perceptible ridge. A short distance north-west of the hill there is also a seldom used, but functional airstrip, called Kinyanguru airstrip. When we built it in the early nineties the workers originally constructed in an L-shape around a big Baobab tree, as it is believed that destroying such a tree brings bad luck, or possibly worse. We had to re-align the airstrip in order to avoid the Baobab. The tree is not there anymore, as it suddenly decided to die.

Coming from Matambwe, there is another road leading to Kinyanguru. Travelling towards Mtemere, there is a turnoff to the left after 7km. The road leads north, crosses the railway line after around 8km and continues towards Kinyanguru Hill and the Mgeta River, which forms the border of the Reserve. It circles the hill to the west and leads up to the airstrip on the Mgeta, joining the road coming up from Kinyanguru station.

The vegetation is scattered acacia bush land, with low-grass-plains towards the north. There are some minor hills close to the road covered with thickets. The area is very rich in wildlife and the authors must admit that Kinyanguru is one of their favourable spots, which they only very reluctantly share with the world. In the open grasslands herds of plains game such as wildebeest, zebra, impala, eland, buffalo and giraffe are plentiful. Lions are also frequently sighted and visitors may even be lucky enough to spot kudu, big packs of wild dogs and the odd leopard, which is a common resident of the many thickets and riverine forests along the Mgeta. Kinyanguru is a heaven for warthogs. It contains – we think - possibly one of the densest concentrations anywhere in Africa of these odd looking animals. In the dry season, when the grass is low, the visitor is rarely out of sight of warthogs. In the early morning and late evening groups of its nocturnal counterpart, the bush pig, are frequently encountered.

To the north of the area across the Mgeta River lies Gonabis, a community wildlife management area, which forms one ecosystem with Kinyanguru. Depending on climatic conditions big herds of wildebeest, buffalo and zebra cross and recross the Mgeta in a kind of local migration in search of green grazing. In very dry periods it might seem that most of the game on the Selous side has gone except the odd resident wildebeest bull standing under an acacia tree and waiting for his harem to return .

The Mgeta itself forms a distinct ecosystem. It is a permanent river with steep banks, around 10m to 25m wide. Its fringes are covered with dense riverine vegetation. It is not very deep and in the dry season can be

Left: Female warthogs with young

crossed on foot. It dries out during prolonged periods of drought like that, for example, at the end of 2003. The crocodiles then survive in tiny pools and caves in the river walls or in some river arms on the south bank which are completely overgrown and full of rotting trees which have fallen in these mysterious black waters. The large population of big crocodiles is connected with the Ruvu River and these crocs take a heavy toll of the adjacent villages. In 2000 and 2001 a total of 22 people were killed by them of which 11 came from just one village.

Walking along the Mgeta is a fantastic experience. A guide is essential and visitors have to be very careful not to get too close to the numerous elephants in the riverine forests. Even lions can be found sleeping on the game trodden path along the river bank. The walk can lead you close to all the animals listed and in addition, especially when it is very dry, the chances of seeing bushbuck, red duiker and colobus monkeys are good. Large water birds like storks and herons can be observed in the water. Hammerkops with their large nests are numerous.

It is recommended that visitors enquire about road conditions before driving to the Kinyanguru area. This is because of the black cotton soil on some stretches of road, which make them impassable after heavier rainfall. Permission has been granted by the Ministry to build two tented camps and one lodge in the area, but construction has not started and they will not open before 2007.

Walking and Trekking in the Wilderness

There are some national parks in East Africa where you can watch elephants and lions in comfort from the veranda of a lodge whilst sipping tea or a gin & tonic. In many such places the animals are deliberately attracted to artificial water holes to enable tourists to see them. Alternatively, tourists are driven around in a minibus and must experience the difficulty of trying to photograph a lion without half a dozen other vehicles in the background.

The Selous is different! It is one of Africa's last untamed wildernesses and in its southern parts there are still places where no man has ever set foot. It is Africa as Livingstone saw it, where the minibus is an unknown feature and wildlife abounds. The Tanzanian Wildlife Division intends to keep it this way and is seeking to maintain its character as a wilderness reserve, difficult as this may be.

The adventure-seeking traveller can explore this wilderness on foot, a privilege that is possible in very few parks in Africa. The visitor can join a walking safari while staying in one of the camps. Such a walk usually begins in the early morning and lasts for several hours, and an armed game scout always accompanies the group. More adventurous are the trekking safaris, which last for several days. A small group of trekkers start from base camp with guides and a game scout. In the evening they set up their tents at a scenic spot and move on the following morning. Trekking is actually the best way to experience the heartbeat of the Selous and is organised by some camps. Independent trekking is in principle possible and can be arranged with the Selous office in Dar es Salaam. It is not a low-budget affair, however, and needs considerable preparation, equipment and experience.

Left: Typical walking safari encounter
Next page: Lioness and lion

TZR 4933

ACCESS TO THE RESERVE AND SOME ADVICE

By Road

A four-wheel drive vehicle is obligatory for driving inside the Reserve or even reaching it. The south-eastern access is an approx. 240km drive (seven to eight hours) from Dar es Salaam via Kibiti, Mkongo and Mloka to Mtemere gate. The 133km stretch from Dar es Salaam to Kibiti is mainly tarmac and the next 33km to Mkongo, where the route turns right (West) is an all-weather dirt surface track. The remaining 74km can become temporarily impassable during heavy rains. Between Mloka village and Mtemere gate the Selous Mbega Camp is situated in a beautiful dense riverine forest.

The northern access is a 350km drive (seven to nine hours) from Dar es Salaam to the Matambwe gate. It is 190km on tarmac road to Morogoro and from the town centre you take the road in the direction of the Teachers Training College. Shortly after the College there is a right turn which is the road to Kisaki. There is also a shortcut 15km ahead of Morogoro to the left

Left: Be prepared to push if it rains!

from the main tarmac road, just before reaching the ORYX filling station. This shortcut joins the main road to Kisaki about 20km from Morogoro.

This is a delightful scenic route through the Uluguru Mountains. The sometimes steep and rocky road will take between three and five hours to drive, depending on its maintenance status which may not be good. In the rainy season, river crossings in the final leg of the route may be impassable. Permanent bridges or drifts are currently being constructed with financial assistance from Germany.

A short drive after crossing a river by an old concrete bridge in the village of Mvuha, a signboard shows the way to a campsite on the right, where tourists with camping equipment can spend the night, at low cost (US$5) before entering the Game Reserve. From the campsite, located at the Mambarawe Ridge (the foothills of the Uluguru Mountains), visitors have a splendid view over the Northern Selous. The hills invite you to watch the sunrise, and two creeks with small waterfalls and dense tropical vegetation are waiting for exploration and offer a refreshing bath. Village game scouts of the JUKUMU society guard the site, which is part of the Community

Wildlife Management Scheme. Facilities include water from a clean mountain creek, toilets and shower rooms. Firewood is available to buy. Visitors should register at the scout station uphill. Ten km after Kisaki village, just outside the Selous boundary, on the right side of the road is situated the Sable Mountain Lodge, which is operated under a lease agreement with the communities. It has been built in the hills that straddle the road to the south, from where the visitor has a scenic view over the Selous and the Uluguru mountains. The GPS coordinates for the entrance gates are: Matambwe (S 0732054 E 0374601) and Mtemere (S 074501 E 0381247).

Another access route for the more adventure minded traveller starts from the road south of Mikumi village. It meanders through the wooded Southern Mikumi National Park, finally follows the Tazara and ends in Kisaki village. This road was reopened in 1990, but is not regularly maintained and becomes impassable when it rains. Visitors who wish to use it must first enquire about its condition from Mikumi National Park or the Selous office.

Left: Breeding herd
Top: Rhino sculpture in Sand Rivers

By Plane

The airstrips at Beho Beho (S 074005 E 0375539), Mbuyu (S 074048 E 0380520), Rufiji River Camp/Mtemere (S 074501 E 0381247), Sand Rivers Selous/Kibambawe (S 074445 E 0380004), Selous Safari Camp (S 074127 E 0380821) and Stiegler's Gorge (S 075000 E 0374700) can all be reached by chartered light aircraft from Dar es Salaam within an hour. Daily scheduled flights are provided by Coastal Aviation (tel. +255-22-2843293) and ZAN Air (+255-24-2233670 or 2233768). Foxes African Safaris (tel. +255-741/4/8-237422) operate scheduled flights three times a week and also offer combinations with Mikumi, Ruaha and Katavi National Parks as well as the Southern Highlands. Scheduled flights between Dar es Salaam cost around US$120 per single trip. These flights do not operate when most camps are closed in April and May.

By Train

The Tazara railway passes through the northern edge of the Reserve. Trains run three times a week (first class ticket costs US$ 7 one way) and it takes about 4 to 5 hours to reach Kinyanguru, Fuga or Matambwe stations in the Selous or Kisaki station. Express trains stop only at Kisaki and Kinyanguru. Westbound tickets should be bought a few days in advance, but when returning to Dar tickets can be bought at the station. Eastbound trains are often late, but the station master knows the estimated time of arrival. When travelling to the Selous by train visitors must be collected by a vehicle from the camp in which they are booked. In all cases prior arrangements have to be made, and it should be noted that not all camps pick up visitors from the train. There are neither tourist facilities nor transport available at the Reserve's headquarters, Matambwe, contrary to what one popular guidebook for low-budget travellers states. Foxes African Safaris (tel. +255-(0)741/4/8-237422) run a special train ("Safari Express") on Sundays, Tuesdays and Fridays which continues to Mikumi and Udzungwa National Parks. Single trips to the Selous cost US$120, return US$180.

Camping

Camping is allowed in the Reserve at two designated campsites. The sites are: Beho Beho bridge and Lake Tagalala.

Information about camping in the Reserve can be obtained from the Chief Warden or at Matambwe or Mtemere Stations. Visitors are generally advised to make use of the services of a game scout for general assistance and for protection. All camping sites are frequented by dangerous animals. This is normally not a problem, if visitors behave reasonably and fortunately no accident has so far occurred.

Camping fees (US$20 per person per day in addition to the entry fees) are payable in advance at the Selous office in Dar es Salaam or at the gates. The camper must bring a kerosene or gas stove for cooking. Small campfires are allowed but with collected dead wood only. Water is obtainable nearby at most times but must be filtered and preferably boiled. For preference, drinking water should be brought in, as most rivers and all the lakes are murky. Simple toilets have been erected at the sites, and all waste must be taken back out of the Reserve.

No camping is permitted outside of the official camping sites, but arrangements can be made for special camping sites in the Mtemere-Manze zone on payment of the appropriate fee (US$40 per person per day in addition to the entry fees). Visitors are required to contact the Reserve management for details.

The JUKUMU camping site (US$5 per person per night) is two hours drive away from Matambwe on the road towards Morogoro on the left. It is called Kilengezi and

---

Left: Sunset over Rufiji

the headquarter of the village scouts who conserve and manage the Wildlife Management Area north of the Reserve. Coming from Dar it is on the right (north), about 500m from the road and the turn off is clearly marked by a large signboard. Scouts stay at the station around the clock and arriving late is not problem.

Hints for Motorists

Visitors coming by car have to bring their fuel from Dar es Salaam, Morogoro or Kibiti. There are no repair facilities in the Reserve. Vehicles must be 4-wheel drive. Drivers are advised to carry essential items such as tools, spare tyre, tyre repair kit, shovel, panga and drinking water. In the event of a breakdown in the Reserve stay with your vehicle and wait for another car to come along. If you must go for help in the case of a real emergency always follow the designated roads and tracks and remember that even in such a case you should not walk after sunset, as it is very dangerous.

All distances and travel times given in this guide are approximate and should be regarded as indicative only. New sightseeing and anti-poaching tracks are being built by the Reserve's management, and they can not all be described here. Gates are open from 6 a.m. to 6 p.m.

The best season to visit

To start with, all seasons are best only different! The most pleasant time to visit the Selous is during the cool season from the end of June until October. The drier it gets the more areas are burnt, and the bare burnt grounds look a bit depressing to some visitors. On the other hand the animals are not dispersed as they are during and after the rains. They have to come to the water regularly, and this is therefore the best time to observe game in bigger numbers, even in concentrations. It can already be pleasantly cool in May and June, depending on the year. The rainy season in the Selous is normally from November to May, although there is a drier spell in January and February. This is also a beautiful time to visit as the trees and flowers are blossoming and everywhere it is green. Every old Africa hand knows, however, that the rains are notoriously unreliable. Showers occur in the dry season and drought in the wet season. If you have doubts, enquire about the road conditions before you travel! It is only during the heavy rains, normally from the end of March to May, that the Reserve is inaccessible and most tourist camps are closed. Nevertheless some may accept visitors even during the rainy season when it is very possible that there will be lengthy dry spells.

Left: Beho Beho Lodge
Next page: All prepared for dinner after river cruise at Sand Rivers

ACCOMODATION

TENTED CAMPS AND LODGES

Beho Beho
P.O. Box 2261
Dar es Salaam
Tel: +255 22 2600352/4
Fax: +255 22 2600347
behobeho@acexnet.com
obhotel@acexnet.com
www.behobeho.com

Selous Impala Camp
P.O. Box 40569
Dar es Salaam
Tel: +255 22 2452005/6
Fax: +255 22 2452004
+255 744 813940
info@adventurecamps.co.tz
reservations@adventurecamps.co.tz
www.adventurecamps.co.tz

Selous Mbega Camp
P.O. Box 23443
Dar es Salaam
Tel: +255 22 2650250
+255 748 624664/748888
+255 744 035530
+255 22 2650251
baobabvillage@raha.com
www.selous-mbega-camp.com

Rufiji River Camp
P.O. Box 13824
Dar es Salaam
Tel: +255 22 2128662/3
Fax: +255 22 2128661
booking@hippotours.com
info@hippotours.com
www.hippotours.com

Sable Mountain Lodge
P.O. Box 40525
Dar es Salaam
Tel:+255 22 2110507
+255 741 323318
Fax: +255 22 2151106
tentview@intafrica.com
safariscene@intafrica.com
www.saadani.com
www.selouslodge.com

Sand Rivers Selous
Nomad Tanzania
P.O. Box 681, Usa River
Arusha
Tel: +255 27 2553819/20
Fax: +255 27 2553830
info@nomad.co.tz
www.nomad-tanzania.com
www.sand-rivers-selous.com

Selous Safari Camp
P.O. Box 1192
Dar es Salaam
Tel: +255 22 2128485/2134802
+255 744 353555
Fax: +255 22 2112794
nicky@selous.com
reservations@selous.com
www.selous.com

Left top: Rufiji River Camp
Left bottom: Impala Camp
Next page: Selous Safari Camp
Page 120: Impala ram

SELOUS GAME RESERVE FEE STRUCTURE (2005):

TYPE OF FEE	CITIZENS	NON-CITIZENS
A. PERMIT FOR ENTRY OF EACH PERSON	**TSHS**	**US $**
1. On or above the age of 16 years	1,500	30
2. Between the age of 6 and 15 years	500	5
3. On or below the age of 5 years	Free	Free
B. PERMIT FOR EACH MOTOR VEHICLE		
1. Tare weight up to 2,000 kg	5,000	30
2. Tare weight between 2,000 kg and 7,000 kg	50,000	150
3. Above 7,000 kg	100,000	200
C. PERMIT FOR CAMPING IN ANY CAMPING SITE PER DAY		
(1) ON ESTABLISHED CAMPING SITES		
I. Each person on or above 16 years	1,000	20
II. Each person between 6 and 15 years	100	5
III. Children on or below the age 5 years	Free	Free
(2) ON SPECIAL CAMPING SITES		
I. Each person on or above 16 years	2,000	40
II. Each person between 6 and 15 years	100	10
III. Children on or below the age of 5 years	Free	Free
D. GUIDE FEES		
1. For the service of an official guide	5,000	10
2. For the service of an official guide, who accompanies tourists outside official working hours	7,500	15
3. For the service of an official guide on walking safaris	5,000	20
4. For the service of a game guard on camping areas NB: it is mandatory for all campers to have a game guard in the camping areas	5,000	20

EXPLANATIONS:

- Entry fees and permit fees for vehicles are per 24 hours (e.g. from 9.00 am until 9.00 am the following day)
- Citizen fee for motor vehicles means Tanzanian registered vehicles. Non-citizen fee means foreign registered vehicles. A non-citizen entering the Reserve in a Tanzania registered vehicle pays the lower citizen fee for this vehicle and vice-versa.
- Guide fees are per guide irrespective how many people are guided.

You must obtain an official receipt for every payment. Entry fees may be subject to change without prior notice, and up-to-date information can be obtained from camp and tour operators or from the Selous administration. Please remember that the fees are channelled back into the Reserve and this is your contribution towards conservation of wildlife.

The Reserve's staff are always pleased to offer advice or render assistance to visitors. If you have anything to report or if you have any complaints or suggestions, please do not hesitate to write to the Chief Warden or consult with the Sector Warden at Matambwe.

The visitor can contact the Selous Ofice at the "Ivory Room", Nyerere Road (at Chang'ombe turnoff on the way to the airport), Dar es Salaam for all enquiries. Postal address:

Chief Warden - Selous Game Reserve - P.O. Box 25295 – Dar es Salaam
Tel: ++255-22-866064 - Fax: ++255-22-861007 – email: scp@africaonline.co.tz

SOME RULES TO REMEMBER

Every visitor to a conservation area should try to minimise the impact of tourism on the environment. In particular the following rules must be observed:

- Do not enter the Reserve without permission. The gates at Mtemere and Matambwe are the official entry points to the Northern Sector. Entry at any other place is an offence. All visitors have to pay the respective entry fees. Fee receipts should be kept, as they may be checked again. Visitors to tourist camps pay their fee at the camp.
- Do not use Reserve boundaries or boundary tracks in any way without valid entry permit. This would be an offence, as they are inside the Reserve.
- Do not speed. The speed limit is 50km. Wild animals often cross or rest on the roads, and this limit is set to protect both them and you. The recommended speed for viewing is 25km - you will see much more at this speed. Any accident involving a wild animal has to be reported at the first opportunity.
- Do not approach too closely or disturb animals including birds. Please keep quiet so as to encourage them to have confidence in humans. Never blow your horn or bang on the doors.
- Do not make any noise or create a disturbance, which might offend other visitors.
- Do not pick any flowers or uproot, cut or destroy any vegetation.
- Do not bring any wild or domesticated animals or plants into the Reserve.
- Do not remove anything indigenous to the Reserve.
- Do not leave anything behind except your tracks. Take your litter back with you.
- Do not light any fires or discard burning cigarette ends or matches.
- Do not drive after dark.
- Do not bring any type of firearm or any other weapon into the Reserve, as this will lead to criminal prosecution.
- Do not drive off the roads. Please keep on authorised roads and tracks.
- Do not get out of your vehicle within 200m of any wild animal.
- Do not move more than 25m away from a car unless accompanied by an armed game scout or an authorised guide.

BIBLIOGRAPHY

A detailed tourist map of the Northern Sector has been produced by the authors with GTZ. Please enquire from your tourist lodge or the local bookstores.

The website of the GTZ Wildlife Programme in Tanzania contains many specialized papers on the Selous including a bird list and a bibliography for downloading:
www.wildlife-programme.gtz.de/wildlife

OTHER BOOKS PUBLISHED BY GALLERY PUBLICATIONS

A Taste of Zanzibar - Zarina Jafferji & Javed Jafferji
A mouth-watering selection of Zanzibar's finest recipes to set your taste buds tingling with memories of your stay in Zanzibar.

Dhow Chasing in Zanzibar Waters - Captain G L Sullivan
An action-packed autobiographical account of the efforts of British naval Captain to help suppress the illegal sea trade in slaves in the Indian Ocean.

Doors of Zanzibar - Mwalim A Mwalim
Celebrates the intricate detail and beauty of Zanzibar's carved wooden doors, exploring Indian, Arabic and Swahili influences. Illustrated with stunning photographs.

Historical Zanzibar - Romance of the Ages - Professor Abdul Sheriff & Javed Jafferji
Illustrated account of Zanzibar's turbulent past, with archive photographs of the slave and ivory trade, life in the palace, the Shortest War in History and colonial rule.

Images of Lamu - Elie Losleben & Javed Jafferji
Images of Lamu is a photographic book of the culture, history and architecture of Kenya's northern archipelago. A UNESCO World Heritage Site, Lamu has captivated travelers for generations.

Images of Zanzibar - Bethan Rees Jones & Javed Jafferji
Glossy coffee-table book packed with stunning photographs from across Zanzibar and Pemba, including Stone Town, landscapes, beaches, culture, and aerial shots.

Life of Frederick Courtenay Selous - J.G Millais
Autobiography of the famous hunter, explorer, naturalist, patriot and pioneer, providing a glimpse into the life of an extraordinary Englishman in the heyday of colonial Africa.

Lake Manyara National Park - Graham Mercer & Javed Jafferji
A park often overlooked by passing visitors.This book should put Manyara back where it belongs, among the very best of Tanzania's wonderful sanctuaries. Excellent Photographs.

Memoirs of an Arabian Princess from Zanzibar - Emily Reute
Written by Princess Salme, who eloped with a German trader, this autobiography provides an absorbing account of life in the harem and the palaces during the sultanate rule.
Also available in French, Italian, Spanish and German

Magic of Zanzibar - Gemma Pitcher & Javed Jafferji
A handy pocket-sized book of photographs for visitors to take home. Zanzibar's architecture, natural history, culture and colourful people are all depicted in full colour.

Mikumi National Park - Graham Mercer & Javed Jafferji
For too long Mikumi has been one of East Africa's most underrated parks. This book should change all that. It includes a fascinating history of the area as well as many insights into the park itself. Superb photographs.

Ngorongoro Conservation Area - Graham Mercer & Javed Jafferji
What more can be written about this jewel in Tanzania's tourist-attraction crown? Quite a lot, as this book shows. Much of the information will be new to many people, and the whole Conservation Area is covered, not just the famous Crater. Top class photographs to match.

Serengeti National Park - Graham Mercer & Javed Jafferji
The Serengeti, with its astonishing seasonal migration, is the world's most famous national park, yet this new guide book treats it in a refreshingly individual and interesting way, made even more interesting by up-to-date information on the park and its wonderful wildlife. Illustrated by excellent photographs.

Safari Elegance - Amanda Harley & Javed Jafferji
Capturing the spirit of romance and adventure in the heart of the African wilderness, Safari Elegance celebrates the best of Kenya's safari design against the dramatic backdrop of the country's diverse landscape. Created as havens of elegance and style, the exclusive tented camps and lodges blend effortlessly with the natural beauty of an ancient land steeped in history and woven with legends.

Safari Kitchen - Amanda Harley & Javed Jafferji
A glossy coffee table style cookbook featuring the very best of Kenya's safari cuisine - from breakfast in the bush, to sundowners and sumptuous dinners served in elegant surroundings. Fabulous still-life shots of prepared dishes are combined with images of unique dining experiences in the heart of the wilderness, and interior design shots of the lodges and camps.

Safari Living - Gemma Pitcher & Javed Jafferji
Glossy coffee table book exploring the neglected area of Tanzania's design heritage, celebrating the style of the country's luxury safari lodges and private homes.

Safari Living Recipes - Gemma Pitcher and Javed Jafferji
Accompanying 'designer' cookbook featuring handpicked recipes from Tanzania's top safari lodges and camps.

Simply Zanzibar - Gemma Pitcher & Javed Jafferji
A lush, full colour coffee table book celebrating the unique visual appeal of the Spice Islands Zanzibar and Pemba. Hundreds of full colour photographs accompanied by informative text.

Sowing the Wind, Pemba before the Revolution - Maulid M Haji
Autobiographical novel exploring life and politics through the eyes of its central character, Maulid, in the turbulent years leading up to independence, an d the subsequent revolution in 1964.

Swahili Style - Elie Losleben & Javed Jafferji
Swahili Style covers the design and architecture of the Swahili Coast of Kenya and Tanzania, featuring exclusive properties and private homes that have taken their inspiration from the old stone towns and coral palaces of the Indian Ocean coastline.

Swahili Kitchen - Elie Losleben & Javed Jafferji
Swahili Kitchen features the best of Swahili cooking as served in the area's best lodges. From the beaches of Kenya and Tanzania, full menus using island spices and fresh Indian Ocean catch are a perfect way to remember East Africa.

Ruaha National Park - Graham Mercer & Javed Jafferji

Ruaha is one of East Africa's finest parks and one of its wildest. Why do so many "old Africa hands love it?". This book and its wonderful photographs might provide the answer.

Tanzania African Eden - Graham Mercer & Javed Jafferji

Beautifully illustrated and well-written tribute to Tanzania's many attractions, in coffee table format – a wonderful gift for anyone living in Tanzania, visiting it or for armchair travelers who want to experience this astonishing part of East Africa at second-hand.

The Krazy Kanga Book - Pascal Bogaert

A distinctly off-beat book looking at some of the more bizarre aspects of East Africa's favourite garment - the kanga. Illustrated with lively and entertaining sketches showing the endless uses for kanga and how to wear them.

Tippu Tip, His Career in Zanzibar and Central Africa - Dr Heinrich Brode

New edition of Dr Brode's highly readable account of the life and times of Zanzibar's most notorious slave trader, his relationships with explorers Livingstone, Cameron, Stanley and Wissman, and his role in the international expedition to rescue Emin Pasha.

Tarangire National Park - Graham Mercer & Javed Jafferji

For years Tarangire was almost unknown except to a select group of "old Africa hands", who were happy to have the place to themselves. That has now changed, and an increasing number of tourists are discovering the park each year. This book, written by someone who first visited Tarangire in 1977, should help to explain why. As should the fine photographs by the celebrated Zanzibari photographer Javed Jafferji.

Zanzibar, A Plan for the Historic Stone Town - Francesco Siravo & Stefano Bianca

Packed with historical information, plans photographs and illustrations, this reference book takes a detailed look at Zanzibar's history and architecture, and the future preservation of Stone Town.

Zanzibar in Contemporary Times - Robert Nunez Lyne
Focuses on the nineteenth century, detailing the consolidation of Omani Arab power from the Gulf to Zanzibar, the arrival of the British, and the struggle against the slave trade.

Zanzibar Stone Town, An Architectural Exploration
Professor Abdul Sheriff & Javed Jafferji
A pocket-sized guide examining the unique blend of architectural styles that make up Zanzibar's historic quarter, illustrated with sketches and colour photographs.

Zanzibar Style - Gemma Pitcher & Javed Jafferji
A sumptuous full colour coffee table book celebrating the natural style of the island's inhabitants, exploring themes inspiring Zanzibar's architecture and interior design.
Available in Spanish, French, Italian and German

Zanzibar Style Recipes - Gemma Pitcher & Javed Jafferji
Accompanying 'designer' cookbook featuring a selection of dishes from Zanzibar's upmarket hotels and resorts.

Zanzibar Tales - George Bateman
A lively and entertaining translation of Swahili folktales passed down from generation to generation.

Zanzibar - An Essential Guide - Amanda Harley & Javed Jafferji
All the essential information for visitors seeking to discover this tropical paradise. Lush spice plantations, historic ruins, the narrow streets of Stone Town and pristine beaches lapped by the turquoise waters of the Indian Ocean are but a few of the gems waiting to be discovered. Fringed by colourful coral reefs, Zanzibar also offers an underwater Eden for divers and snorkellers.

All books distributed by:
Zanzibar Gallery, Mercury House, P.O. Box 3181, Zanzibar,
e-mail: gallery@swahilicoast.com

INDEX

About the Authors

Dr. Rolf D. Baldus headed the Selous Conservation Programme between 1987 and 1993. Since 1998 he has been GTZ Government Advisor on Community Based Wildlife Management, and he coordinates the German priority sector "Natural Resources" in Tanzania. He has written over 100 publications on conservation in Africa.

Dr. Ludwig Siege was Coordinator of the Selous Conservation Programme from 1994 to 2003 after which he returned to work in GTZ-Headquarters in Germany. Today he manages a development project in Madagascar.

About the Photographer

Javed Jafferji studied photography, film and television in the UK, before returning to Tanzania to publish over thirty books on East Africa. His work has been published in national and international newspapers and magazines. He has held exhibitions in London, Paris, Berlin and Pakistan as well as Tanzania.

Javed also publishes 'The Swahili Coast' magazine to promote eco-tourism in Tanzania and 'Tanzania Travel & Tourism Directory' the official tourism directory published in association with Tourism Confederation of Tanzania and Tanzania Tourist Board, He also manages a photography and graphic design company, and runs a shop, Zanzibar Gallery, which sells gifts, clothes, books and antiques.